this author, a biblical text that is often read in rather dry manner comes alive again.

Dr. Bob Cornwall
Pastor of Central Woodward Christian Church, Troy, MI
Author, Editor, and Activist

c

PRAISE FOR *TRANSFORMING ACTS*

"Acts of the Apostles is good news for those who want to join head, heart, and hands in an intellectually-solid, spiritually-inspiring, and socially-active faith," says Dr. Epperly as you begin a journey of discovery. If your church community is looking for ways to be relevant, to reach out, to live "gospel lives," this book is for you; if you are seeking a guide that will help you understand the gospel message in broad, affirming, yet life-challenging ways, this book can be that guide; if you've almost given up on religious institutions but know that there is something real, vital and transformative about God and faith; this book will supply you with a refreshing glimpse of a vibrant, living faith. Whether you consider yourself churched or "spiritual but not religious," you will find stimulating ideas and challenging thoughts that will assist and affirm your journey of belief, question, doubt and seeking more. Dr. Epperly is a spiritual guide for a new generation of seekers and believers. To read *Transforming Acts* is to go on a journey with a deeply-attuned, thoughtful and progressive thinker and theologian.

Rev. Kathy Harvey Nelson
Director of the Center for Leadership Development
Lancaster Theological Seminary, Lancaster, PA

Reading the Book of Acts, with Bruce Epperly's *Transforming Acts* at hand, reminds you that what's old is new wherever the Spirit addresses the church. This book will be a helpful companion for devotional reading, small group Bible study, or preaching preparation. As Christians learn to relocate themselves in a 21st Century spiritual world that is becoming more like that of the 1st Century, we can find renewed hope in the abiding relevance of the gospel by reading this fresh work.

Rev. Dr. George A. Mason, Senior Pastor
Wilshire Baptist Church, Dallas, Texas

Transforming Acts is a magnificent book! Drawing from a remarkable range of sources, Dr. Epperly presents the Book of Acts in a manner that is both downright compelling and remarkably relevant. If anyone is discouraged with the current state of the institutional church, this is the book to read. The author presents a vision of a compelling community, one with the power to effect necessary change in a broken world. The book strikes a wonderful balance between necessary academic background and a heartfelt vision of the possibilities and potential of the community that seeks to follow Jesus, i.e. the church. I recommend it highly.

Rev. Dr. Robert R. LaRochelle
Pastor, Second Congregational Church, UCC
Manchester, Connecticut

When I was in seminary, there was a great emphasis on producing clergy with positive attitudes and joy-filled ministries. Bruce Epperly has written a book that not only aids in studying Acts but also in producing positive attitudes and joy-filled ministries and lives. Dr. Epperly uses the Acts of the Apostles to open our hearts to acts of our own that are full of love, transformation, and praise.

Throughout this book, the reader is encouraged and challenged to jump fences, pull down walls and realize that we "could be the answer to someone's prayer." This book is an inspiration to Christians in today's world! This is a book I could use in small groups and give to people who are struggling in their faith and spirituality.

Rev. Shauna Hyde, Pastor
author of *Fifty Shades of Grace* and *Victim No More!*

Over the course of time many have treated the Book of Acts as simply a historical record of the early church or a blue print for church organization and practice. In his reading of Acts, Bruce Epperly conceives of it as being gospel for a postmodern age. It offers good news that the Spirit of God is alive and active in our midst, transforming lives and the world itself. It is, he suggests, a word of encouragement to postmodern Christians, who live in a pluralistic context, to let the Spirit lead us on to new spiritual adventures in a world that God loves in Jesus. Yes, in the hands of

TRANSFORMING ACTS:

ACTS OF THE APOSTLES AS A 21ST CENTURY GOSPEL

BRUCE G. EPPERLY

Energion Publications
Gonzalez, FL
2013

Cover Design: Henry Neufeld

ISBN10: 1-938434-64-
ISBN13: 978-1-938434-64-8

Library of Congress Control Number: 2013942955

Energion Publications
P. O. Box 841
Gonzalez, FL 32560

850-525-3916
energionpubs.com
pubs@energion.com

A WORD

OF THANKSGIVING

Hymn-writer Al Carmines' words, "For the giver, for the gift, Praise! Praise! Praise!" rings through my mind as I pen my final words of this text. I believe God is alive and well in the church, calling us to new visions and giving us the energy to faithfully fulfill our vision in this time and place. God's vision for my life, so far as I can intuit, has been inspired by many people: my mother and father, Loretta and Everett Epperly; pastors John Akers, George "Shorty" Collins; teachers Marie Fox, Richard Keady, John Cobb, David Griffin, Bernard Loomer; academic and spiritual colleagues Ed Aponte, Jay McDaniel, Monica Coleman, Doug Pagitt, Brian McLaren, Catherine Keller, Helene Russell, Ron Allen, Kent Ira Groff, J. Philip Newell, and Kathy Harvey Nelson; friends Anna Rollins and Patricia Adams Farmer; and, of course, my family, Kate Gould Epperly, Matt Epperly, Ingrid Lemmey Epperly, and my "grand-boys" Jack and Jamie. I am grateful to Dean and Provost Philip Clayton and President Jerry Campbell for the opportunity to spend Fall 2012 teaching and writing at Claremont School of Theology and Claremont Lincoln University. At Claremont School of Theology and Claremont Lincoln University, I had the opportunity to be part of a truly vital seminary and graduate school, attentive to the role of interreligious partnerships in healing the world. I am also thankful to Henry and Jody Neufeld at Energion Publications for their commitment to boundary-breaking scholarship to transform the church.

This text had its inception in a series of twelve sermons I preached between May 13 and August 12, 2012 at First Christian Church, Falls Church, Virginia. I am grateful to Senior Pastor Kathleen Kline Moore for her generosity in turning her pulpit over to me during her sabbatical and to an excellent pastoral staff and lay leadership that took care of the many details of ministry so that I could devote myself to what I do best: preach, teach, mentor, and pastor.

I write out of my love for seminarians, pastors, lay leaders, as well as my hope that a vital progressive-evangelical-emerging-spirit-centered church will burst forth and take its role as God's partner in healing the Earth. As you read this text, I invite you to open to God's dynamic spirit and take your place as a companion in a never-ending story of grace, healing, love, and transformation.

Bruce Epperly
Rosh Hashanah 2012
(A Blessed New Year and Time for New Beginnings
for Church and Synagogue)

TABLE OF CONTENTS

ONE

A POSTMODERN GOSPEL?

While Paul was waiting for them in Athens, he was deeply distressed to see that the city was full of idols. So he argued in the synagogue with certain Jews and the devout persons, and also in the marketplace every day with those who happened to be there. Also some Epicurean and Stoic philosophers debated with him. Some said, "What does this babbler want to say?" Others said, "He seems to be a proclaimer of foreign divinities." (This was because he was telling the good news about Jesus and the resurrection.) So they took him and brought him to the Areopagus and asked him, "May we know what this new teaching is that you are presenting? It sounds rather strange to us, so we would like to know what it means." Now all the Athenians and the foreigners living there would spend their time in nothing but telling or hearing something new.

Then Paul stood in front of the Areopagus and said, "Athenians, I see how extremely religious you are in every way. For as I went through the city and looked carefully at the objects of your worship, I found among them an altar with the inscription, 'To an unknown god.' What therefore you worship as unknown, this I proclaim to you. The God who made the world and everything in it, he who is Lord of heaven and earth, does not live in shrines made by human hands, nor is he served by human hands, as though he needed anything, since he himself gives to all mortals life and breath and all things. From one ancestor he made all nations to inhabit the whole earth, and he allotted the times of their existence and the boundaries of the places where they would live, so that they would search for God and perhaps grope for him and find him—though indeed he is not far from each one of us. For 'In him we live and move and have our being'; as even some of your own poets have said, 'For we too are his offspring.' Since we are God's offspring, we ought not to think that the deity is like gold, or silver, or stone, an image formed by the art and imagination of mortals. While God has overlooked the times of human ignorance, now he commands all people everywhere to repent, because he has fixed a day on which he will have the world judged in righteousness by a man whom he has appointed, and of this he has given assurance to all by raising him from the dead." When they heard of the resurrection of the dead, some scoffed; but others said, "We will hear you again about this." At that point Paul left them. (Acts 17:16-33)

LIVING ACTS

Acts of the Apostles is a living gospel. It is good news for doubters, seekers, and believers who have discovered that their vision of God and the spiritual adventure is too small for the universe revealed in the Hubble telescope, Higgs Boson particles, evolutionary science, and the varieties of global and local spiritual experience. Acts of the Apostles is good news for those who want to join head, heart, and hands in an intellectually-solid, spiritually-inspiring, and socially-active faith. The message of Acts can breathe new life into congregations, inspiring them to go beyond their comfort zones to become agents of divine hospitality and justice. Acts is about experiencing God's Spirit in surprising moments and ordinary places.

In looking at Acts, we discover that the good news of God's all-transforming and all-embracing love resonates with the postmodern emphasis on experience and story-telling. Acts reminds us that our individual stories and the narratives of our communities are as important and as meaningful as the large stories others claim apply to all humankind without exception. In sharing the stories of Paul, Lydia, Philip, Peter, Cornelius, an Ethiopian eunuch, and the healing of an unnamed slave girl, Acts invites us to claim our stories of seeking and finding and seeking again. It challenges us to listen to God's call in the voices of those who have left the church, who find the church irrelevant and intolerant, and who struggle to discover new ways of following Jesus. Today, some of the most ardent seekers of new images of Jesus and healing visions of God are to be found in the church or at its spiritual edges.

Judy knocked on my study door one bright spring day. When she told me that she was going through a spiritual crisis, I suggested that we take a walk in the neighborhood adjoining the seminary where I taught. One of my brightest students, destined to be an inspiring and compassionate pastor or professor, Judy confided that she had lost her spiritual center. "Jesus is still important to me, but I'm struggling with what it means to be a Christian. I no longer find inspiration in liturgical worship and, apart from your classes, no one in the church or seminary talks about prayer and meditation or has a clue about how to integrate spiritual practices into congregational life. When I hear what some of my fellow Christians say about God and salvation, even in my own congregation, I'm embarrassed by their uncritical belief that God's in control of everything that happens and that God's plan includes causing cancer, birth defects, and earthquakes that kill thousands of people. I still read the Gospels but I find my inspiration these days in reading the Dalai Lama, the Tao Te Ching, and poets like Denise Levertov and Mary Oliver. I want to be faithful to Jesus, but there are so many spiritual paths today; I wonder how I can be an honest pastor and also share my spiritual life with my congregation."

Later that week, I ran into Matt, a layperson who had sat in on a few of my classes. He, too, was struggling with his faith. Like Judy, he was in search of what Brian McLaren describes as a "new kind of Christianity."[1] He had found the worship at his mainstream congregation uninspiring and had begun to attend a megachurch on the outskirts of Lancaster, Pennsylvania. As we sat in the Adirondack chairs at Franklin and Marshall College, Matt confided: "I don't know what to do. I like the sermons at my home church, but worship is lifeless. The folks seem to be in a rut and don't want any surprises or displays of emotion. Singing *How Great Thou Art* is as bold as these people get! In contrast, the big church sure has

---

1 Brian McLaren, *A New Kind of Christianity* (San Francisco: Harper One, 2011).

spirit, and I love the praise band and congregational singing, but
the sermons are dreadful. There's a lot of Jesus in the pastor's sermons, and I like that, but lately he's been slamming gay and lesbian
people, social welfare programs, and the use of contraceptives. I
can't talk politics there or say a good word about health care or
gun control. If I mention President Obama's name, folks respond
with contempt and question his faith and patriotism. Despite their
literal understanding of scripture, they don't mention the Prophets
at all and seem to be a local branch of the Republican party! Where
will I find a church that has solid theology and inspiring worship?"

Judy and Matt are representatives of a growing number of
restless seekers within and beyond the church. They want integrity,
authenticity, spirituality, and liveliness. Sadly, many mainstream
and progressive congregations have open theologies but boring
worship, while many conservative churches have lively worship
services but narrow-minded, hate-filled theologies. Moreover, many
congregations are conflicted about what's most important – spirituality or social concern. To some Christians, spirituality implies a
naval gazing retreat from the world. To others, social action without
prayer and meditation is polarizing, trendy, and superficial.

As I reflected on how to introduce the wisdom of Acts of the
Apostles to the readers of this text, I had Judy and Matt along with
countless other seekers in mind. I wanted them to see that they
don't have to choose between action and contemplation; that intel-
lectually solid faith can also be lively and spirit-centered; and that
Christianity can widen, rather than shrink, the circle of welcome
and hospitality. I wanted to share an experiential Christianity that
affirms and embraces the gifts of head, heart, and hands; a faith
that takes prayer and justice-seeking seriously.

I believe that Acts of the Apostles provides a fluid, open-spirited, and holistic faith for twenty-first century people as well as a
vision for congregational transformation and renewal. Anything
can happen to those who follow Jesus. Life is adventurous, surprising, and interesting. Worship leads to mission and mission
challenges narrow-mindedness and self-imposed limitations. For

those who embrace the spirit of Acts of the Apostles, worship will never be boring and every day will be a holy adventure.

ACTS AS A TWENTY-FIRST CENTURY GOSPEL

As I turn the pages of Acts of the Apostles, I am tempted to exclaim "It's déjà vu all over again!" The world of the twenty-first century and the world of the first century look surprisingly similar. The author of Acts, most likely the author of the Gospel of Luke, was a keen observer of the spiritual landscape of his own time. As he pondered writing the sequel to his gospel account of Jesus' life and ministry, I imagine that he saw God's presence in the adventures of Jesus' first followers as they journeyed into the Mediterranean world. I suspect that he experienced first-hand the pluralism, uncertainty, relativism, and change that characterized the first decades of the Jesus movement. He had been touched by Jesus and God's Spirit in a way that joined Jewish wisdom, global mission, and mystical experience. He believed that God was alive and moving through our lives, guiding people through dreams, visions, and unexpected ecstatic experiences. He saw God's hand in the ever-expanding circles of the Jesus movement, beginning at the Jerusalem Pentecost and embracing Rome and beyond. As he penned the manuscript we now know as Acts of the Apostles sometime between 70-80 CE, Luke believed that he was part of a never-ending story of divine call and human response, unhindered by ethnicity, geography, or sociology. He visualized a faith with a moving center, initially revolving around Jerusalem but eventually embracing the whole Earth. He might even have imagined Christians like us, centuries later, telling and retelling the stories of Jesus and he wanted to give us a glimpse of how a small group of people were able to transform the world.

Luke saw the Jesus movement emerging in his own "postmodern" world, where old spiritual certainties were being challenged and people craved experiences of the divine to help them face the inevitabilities of aging and mortality. Consider the following descriptions of the first century Jesus movement as they relate to our own particular time. Do they seem familiar? Do they describe some of the challenges we face in our own pluralistic age? The technology differs, and so does our understanding of the universe and the nature of global communication, but we may have more in common with Jesus' first followers than we previously imagined:

» The early church emerged in a pluralistic and multi-religious society, where it had to compete on equal footing with many other religious traditions. Today, we can no longer claim to be a Christian nation, we are multi-religious nation in which anyone with internet or cable television can become a global citizen. Christianity is just one option among many for the majority of young adults and many of their parents.

» The first Christians had to deal with their poor reputation. They were accused by outsiders of misdeeds such as: undermining Jewish identity, teaching lax morals, and worshiping a strange deity whose character was vastly at odds with the Greek and Roman deities. Today's Christians need to respond to the perception, especially among young adults, that our faith is intolerant, reactionary, backward looking, anti-scientific, sexist, and homophobic.

» For Jesus' first followers the world was in flux. Rome was at its pinnacle but soon would be declining. Signs of its ultimate demise were beginning to surface. The old order was dying, not unlike the economic and global transformations which foretell the eclipse of the American empire and the dream of "American exceptionalism."

» Without fully formed doctrines, creeds, or structures, the early church – guided only by their experiences of Jesus and the Holy Spirit, stories about Jesus, and the Hebraic scriptural witness – made it up as it went along, creating new pathways where none had existed before, trying

out new ways of leadership, spirituality, and mission. As
Christians today, we have a tradition of two thousand
years of doctrinal reflection, but may need to be just as
creative in our theological reflection to be faithful to
Christ today. There is no clear orthodoxy to guide our
path and perhaps there never was a fully orthodox faith
affirmed by all Christians, but many orthodox alternatives
among the Christian stories about God, Christ, Spirit,
atonement, and salvation.

These are exciting, but ambiguous times, for active Christians
and spiritual seekers alike. The future we planned on thirty years
ago, maybe even five years ago, no longer exists – technologically,
economically, globally, or spiritually – and we must make plans
for surprising and emerging futures, not knowing where the paths
ahead will take us. To some observers, we are on the edge of a Great
Awakening, the emergence of a global Christianity, integrating the
best spiritual practices and philosophical insights of other faith
traditions, science, and non-Christian media and literature to form
"a new kind of Christianity." Following Bishop John Shelby Spong,
they know that "Christianity must change or die."[1] In fact, there is
no alternative: change happens and shapes our lives and faith traditions even when they deny or denounce it. In spite of the challenge
and discomfort of change, our sense of disorientation may be good
news, for it calls us to honor the past and venture creatively toward
the future with Christ as our companion. Beyond disorientation
and dislocation, surprises of grace await as we lean forward to new
horizons of faithful adventure.

LIVING IN THE AREOPAGUS

In the mid 1970's, when my teacher John Cobb penned his
classic *Christ in a Pluralistic Age*, his vision of a growing Christianity,

---

1 John Shelby Spong, *Christianity Must Change or Die: A Bishop Speaks
to Believers in Exile* (San Francisco: HarperOne, 2009).

inclusive of multiple spiritual and theological paths was revolutionary.[1] Today, Cobb's imaginative vision has become commonplace, especially in urban areas and college communities. Peoples of all faiths and none at all are discovering that they live in a spiritual Areopagus, the marketplace of spiritual practices and competing religious systems. In the age of internet and cable television, this is just as true for Williamsport, Pennsylvania, Bozeman, Montana, Victoria, British Columbia, as it is in Manhattan or Washington DC. Not too long ago, peoples' religious options were more or less limited to various varieties of Protestant, Catholic, or Jew. Even agnostics and atheists framed their objections to God's existence in Jewish or Christian terms, and used the language of the Bible and theological reflection to challenge the existence of God and traditional moral standards

In this second decade of the twenty-first century, many people feel comfortable sampling the varieties of spiritual delicacies available in the spiritual smorgasbord. The possibilities are almost endless for the religious adventurer. There are few signposts to help the pilgrim find her or his way.

Despite its numerical, political, and historical advantages Christianity no longer can command the sole allegiance of twenty-first century persons but must compete on an even playing field with Scientology, *A Course in Miracles*, *The Secret*, the Dalai Lama, and Tai Chi.

The spiritual landscape is rapidly changing and the congregations and religious institutions that expect to flourish in the future must make it up as they go along, embracing the flow of life and the fluidity of doctrines and spiritual practices while affirming the wisdom of their traditions and founders. Consider the following statistics on North American religion garnered by the Pew Forum on Religion and Public Life:

---

1 John B. Cobb, *Christ in a Pluralistic Age* (Westminster/John Knox, 1975).

» Whereas thirty years ago, less than a quarter of Americans noted that they have had mystical experiences, today 50% of Americans admit to having transcendent spiritual experiences (near death experiences, encounters with spiritual beings, or a deep sense of God's presence).

» 30% of Americans state that they practice multiple spiritualities – they go to church and practice Hindu-based yoga; they join Zen Buddhist meditation with congregational leadership; and they practice reiki healing touch and other energy work and participate in Christian healing services. Traditional religious boundaries no longer apply to many of today's spiritual seekers. The quest for authentic and sometimes ecstatic experiences of the divine drives them away from traditional worship services to experience God in embodied spiritual practices (for example, yoga and Tai Chi), silent meditation, and lively dance, movement, and music.

» The fastest growing self-described religious group is not the Mormons, Pentecostals, or Evangelicals, but the "nones" (not the religious order!) but people who are unaffiliated with any religious tradition, but still claim to be spiritually-inclined. Nearly 20% of the American population describe themselves as belonging to no religious tradition; the percentage is much higher among young adults, many of whom have attended church only for weddings and funerals and see the high holidays of Christianity primarily as opportunities for celebration, consumption, and family reunions.[1]

More significant for the future of Christianity, a variety of studies have noted that Christianity is viewed unfavorably by the

---

1 For an excellent summary and analysis of the current religious situation, see Diana Butler Bass, *Christianity After Religion: The End of the Church and the Birth of a New Spiritual Awakening* (San Francisco: HarperOne, 2012).

majority of youth and young adults. Whenever I teach classes in theology – and theology simply involves our vision of God, the world, human life and its goals – I often ask the following question: "What would you think of Christianity, if all you knew about Christianity were headline stories about Qur'an burning pastors, preachers who inaccurately predict the end of the world, televangelists who blame the 9/11 attacks on the World Trade Center, the Pentagon, and the damage caused by Hurricane Katrina on God's punishment of America for its immorality, and activists who protest the teaching of evolution in public schools?" My students typically protest: "I don't believe those things; that's not my religion!" Then I remind them that for the average North American, who has little or no experience of Christianity- and this would be the majority of young adults – this is virtually all they have heard about Christianity in the media. I also point out that when asked to describe Christianity, most young adults use terms like "anti-intellectual," "intolerant," "anti-science," and "punitive." No wonder many young people avoid our sanctuaries and worship services! No wonder so many young people, baptized and nurtured in the church, are no longer able to see the relevance or value of Christian faith in a world of countless spiritual possibilities and ever-increasing personal demands![1]

On any given plane trip I take, I end up having a conversation with someone who describes him or herself as "spiritual but not religious." When the subject of our conversations turns to science, spirituality, healing, and religious and sexual diversity, they are amazed, first, that I am a Christian and, next, that I am a minister of the gospel for whom Christ is the center of my personal and public life. Often, the last place some seekers look for spirituality and wholeness, much less hospitality and embrace of humankind in all its diversity, is in the church, even though this is – or should be – our primary message.

---

1 Gabe Lyons and David Kinnamon, *UnChristian: What a New Generation Thinks of Christianity and Why it Really Matters* (Grand Rapids: Baker Books, 2007).

One-dimensional understandings of Christianity even occur among active Christians. On a recent cross country air flight, my first class seatmate, who attends a congregation pastored by a well-known Christian devotional writer, was astounded when I spoke positively about President Obama, health care reform, and marriage equality. On the other hand, many progressive Christians assume that all evangelical Christians are biblical literalists, social conservatives, and Tea Party members. The wondrous diversity and many "orthodoxies" of Christian history are overlooked by those who define Christianity in terms of one doctrinal or ecclesiastical tradition, assume Christian uniformity, and assert that authentic Christianity can be summarized by the ancient creeds, the four spiritual laws, or a particular view of scripture and planetary history.

What I've said may seem like bad news for the church, but it could be an opportunity for us to re-think our mission and renew our commitment to sharing the good news of an open-spirited, spiritually-sound, intellectually-lively, and socially concerned faith. For those who awaken to the surprising experiences described in Acts of the Apostles, we may be on the verge of a Great Awakening, emerging in the interplay of ancient-future-now spirituality and worship and Christian truth and practice with the profound insights of other faith traditions.

WE ARE ALL THEOPHILUS

The Gospel of Luke and Acts of the Apostles are both addressed to Theophilus. Unknown apart from these texts, scholars speculate that Theophilus might have been a wealthy patron of the church and a Christian of Greek ethnicity. But, one thing we can be sure of is the meaning of the name, Theophilus: it is "God lover." Could it be that the author of Luke and Acts has two images in mind with the salutation – a wealthy patron, recently converted to the faith, and everyone who reads his account of the life of Jesus and his first followers? More than that, "Theophilus" may embrace every seeker who comes upon the story of Jesus. Deep down all of us are guided by the sighs too deep for words, subtly moving us from aimlessness to adventure and meaninglessness to purpose.

Perhaps, Luke wants to remind us that we are part of a larger story, a narrative that includes Jesus and his Jewish parents, Jesus' earthly ministry, and the many-faceted movement that bears his name throughout history. We are apostles, teachers, healers, witnesses, and seekers in our own time, sharing our stories, asking questions, pushing limits, and recreating the faith as our parents and their parents did. We are lovers of God who want to experience greater dimensions of wonder, energy, power, and love to bring life to our churches and healing to our world. Just as Jesus told his own followers that they would do "greater things" than he, Acts reminds us that the days of lively faith are in present and future not just the past (John 14:12). We are the Peters, Pauls, Lydias, Priscillas, and Philips of our time, creating the church's story as we go along, just as our spiritual parents did. We can experience the same signs and wonders and mediate the same power to heal and transform as our parents in the faith.

ACTS AS A PATHWAY TO TRANSFORMATION

When I was a teenager, I recall a commercial sponsored by Kellogg's Corn Flakes that invited the listener to: "try it again – for the first time!" The commercial implied that in a world of fancy tasting cereals, everyone thinks Corn Flakes is bland and boring; but taste it again and you will discover its good honest flavor.

Today, we need to invite seekers – and ourselves – to try the pathway of Jesus and the wisdom of our faith again – for the first time. I believe that Acts can provide guidance for people who are attempting to chart the church's mission for the decades ahead, faithful to the good news of Jesus and open to the insights and challenges of a rapidly changing world. Paul's experience in the marketplace of ideas and spiritual paths can provide wisdom for people seeking to experience God's good news in our pluralistic and postmodern world.

FAITH IN THE MARKETPLACE OF SPIRITUAL MOVEMENTS

The description of Paul's message at the Areopagus rings a familiar bell for twenty-first century North Americans. Paul is sauntering through the marketplace of spiritualities – it could be Cambridge, Ann Arbor, Berkeley, Madison, or Washington DC where I live. He is gazing at the seat of intellectual, political, and spiritual power and prestige. Statues are everywhere, not unlike Washington DC, London, Paris, or Beijing – to gods and heroes, sacred and secular, known and unknown – each portraying a certain vision of human life and ultimate reality. Paul is both amazed and scandalized at the panorama of diverse and conflicting spiritualities.

Jewish by upbringing and theology, Paul is overwhelmed by the thought of people worshiping objects that are less alive than themselves. Perhaps, he is amazed that people still worship gods such as Zeus who are not only promiscuous in their dalliances with human beings but also vindictive, angry, and punitive. Why would anyone worship raw power when you can experience God's love? Why would anyone follow a religion of fear when he or she could experience God's loving acceptance, grace, and companionship? Why would anyone exalt the gods of violence when the prince of peace welcomed them with open arms?

He engages in conversation with some of the local spiritual leaders and philosophers of the city. They don't know quite what to make of his vision of a universal God, whose life cannot be contained by statues or institutions, and whose love was manifest in a suffering savior. "Tell us more," they ask, because like our culture, they lived with gods aplenty – there as many religious options as there are cable or dish television stations.

Paul enters into dialogue, honoring their religiosity, affirming their quest, but suggesting another better alternative, the path of salvation and wholeness pioneered by Jesus of Nazareth who was unjustly crucified, but miraculously resurrected to bring healing and wholeness, transformation, and love to all creation. There is an "unknown God," whose wisdom is luring us forward even when we are unaware of it, and this is the God Paul has experienced through his encounters with Jesus Christ.

Paul does not attack their spiritual quests in all their wild diversity — nor should we condemn the great religions of the world or the new spiritual movements of our own country. The God in whom we live and move and have our being is inspiring every person's religious quest, even those we presume to be misguided and immature. Most people who follow these movements are seeking, like us, to experience meaning, healing, growth, and peace of mind in a complicated world.

What Paul does is affirm that the divinity revealed in Jesus Christ is present — albeit in disguise and hidden — in their quests for meaning and that Christ provides a way to the meaningful, affirmative, and healthy spirituality they seek. Christ is the reality beneath the "statue of the unknown God." What they don't yet know is the power of God that heals the sick and saves the lost and welcomes everyone to God's banquet table!

Paul does something unique in scripture: he quotes directly– and this is the only place in the Bible — from another religious tradition and attributes the qualities of another god to the God of Jesus Christ: using a hymn of another faith, he affirms that "the reality in whom we live and move and have our being" is the Parent of Jesus Christ. God is not partial to one people or punitive but seeks the well-being of all of us. God is as near as the breath we take and God wants us — all of us, friend and stranger, Christian and non-Christian — to have abundant life.

The conversation concludes with some of Paul's dialogue partners scoffing, but others wanting to continue the conversation. "We will hear you again about this," they promise. Our witness as Christians is both a scandal and an invitation. It is offensive to those who worship the gods of power and prejudice. It scandalizes those who can't imagine a faith without fences and boundaries, welcoming male and female, Jew and Greek, friend and enemy, stranger and neighbor, gay and straight.

Our witness is beginning, not the end of the journey; perhaps, Paul learns something important from his Greek companions. In quoting their philosophers, he may have discovered that the Christ he proclaimed was cosmic as well as personal and global as well as local. He may have found that the wisdom of Christ transcended any particular tongue or ethnicity, including his own form of Christianity.

PRACTICAL WISDOM FROM ACTS OF THE APOSTLES

The Areopagus is the postmodern, pluralistic age in which we live. We cannot evade it, deny its significance, or denounce its spiritual impact; rather we must be transformed in relationship with our world. We must seek spiritual, theological, and technological renewal to respond to the innovations in our environment. Here Paul provides practical wisdom for congregations and spiritual leaders.

First, Paul is a keen observer. He doesn't bury his head in the sand, delivering his message to people in the abstract. In the words of psychiatrist-spiritual guide Gerald May, he *pauses, notices, opens, stretches and yields, and responds.*[1] Revelation is always personal and historical, and so is the sharing of the good news of God's love and transformation. Paul's mindfulness, which includes not only his observation of the many Athenian shrines, but also his distress at certain practices, enables him to deliver an authentic and personal message.

When churches open their senses to the varieties of spirituality, culture, and ethnicities in their context, they can truly dialogue with their neighbors. "Christ is the answer" only when we know the nagging questions and deep hungers of those around us. Spiritual maturity emerges from common ground in our current setting, not the abstractions of a timeless message. In fact, the timeless message is always historical, the uncompromised gospel is always contextual, and the eternal truth is always relational and timely.

1 Gerald May, *The Awakened Heart: Opening Yourself to the Love You Need* (San Francisco: HarperSan Francisco, 1991).

Second, Paul affirms a point of contact with his listeners. He is not preaching to a godless world, but a god-filled world. Isaiah proclaims that "the whole earth is filled with God's glory" (Isaiah 6:3). If we live and move and have our being in God, then there are no godless places or people untouched by divine revelation. We may worship things less alive than ourselves, forgetting our fullness as God's beloved children – consumption, nationalism, success, sensuality, scripture, church, and creed – but even in turning toward lesser objects, God is still touching us and luring us toward wholeness. The point of contact shapes our message: Paul uses Greek concepts in the Areopagus and throughout his writings, and his understanding of the extent of God's grace and love is transformed in the process. Sharing good news involves receiving as well as giving. Paul learned something important about God and humankind that illuminated his message to the cultural elites of Athens.

Third, dialogue may include challenge. There is much to affirm in the marketplace of ideas. We can appreciate and employ spiritual practices of other faith traditions as well as various practices from other Christian traditions. But, our dialogue needs to be mindful and critical. For example, I have appreciated the insights of the popular new age text, *The Secret*, especially as these relate to the power of the mind to shape reality.[1] I believe that our thoughts and practices can transform our attitudes and interpretations of life events. However, *The Secret's* assertion that we "create" the events of our lives in their entirety and are somehow responsible for success as failure, health as well as illness, substitutes an omnipotent mind for an omnipotent god. Although our spiritual practices may shape our well-being, cancer, abuse, and natural disaster come upon the spiritual as well as the unenlightened. Today's Christians may appreciate the ardor of fellow Christians, for example, those who affirm the "prosperity gospel," the belief that God wants us to be successful and that our success mirrors the quality of our faith, while critiqu-

1 Rhonda Byrne, *The Secret* (New York:Atria Books/Beyond Words, 2006).

ing the implicit – and explicit – materialism and consumerism in this "gospel" and its temptation to blame the victim for her or his failures. In the case of *The Secret* and the "prosperity gospel," we can affirm the importance of spiritual growth, faith, and positive attitude without assuming an exact cause and effect relationship between our spiritual maturity and our prosperity and health.

Hospitality does not require acceptance, but it does require respect, care, and listening. Paul observed and listened before he spoke to the Athenian intellectuals, shaping his message in such a way that what he learned in Athens enabled him to share the good news in life-changing ways.

TRANSFORMING ACTS

Acts of the Apostles is an adventure in theospirituality, the joining of theological reflection (our vision of God and the world) and spiritual practices that make God come alive for us. Grace abounds and God is constantly calling to us, often in "sighs too deep for words." Our spiritual practices are ways we can pause and open, and then respond to God's call in our lives. The biblical tradition, and most especially the gospels, affirms the role of human decision-making in opening a door for greater intensity and clarity of God's presence in our lives. When we ask, seek, and knock, we gain inspiration and insight and enable God to be more active in our lives and the world.

Acts is an invitation to spiritual practices. While Acts is not a "how-to" book, the words of Acts point to life-changing spiritual disciplines. Accordingly, each chapter will conclude with a spiritual exercise, illuminating the scripture and enabling us to experience the realities Luke is describing in the early Christian community.

Opening to the Spirit. Gerald May sees the practice of *pausing, noticing, opening, stretching* and *yielding,* and *responding* at the heart of our spiritual practices. In this exercise, take some time to reflect on your environment – the context of your work, home life, play, and spirituality. You can do this sitting in a comfortable chair or walking in your neighborhood or near your church or place of employment.

Prayerfully take a few deep breaths, awakening to the presence of God's Spirit in your life. Breathe the Spirit deeply in and exhale into the ambient environment. Slowly notice what's around you – trees, shrubs, flowers, buildings, and people. Take time to consider the people in your environment. What do you know of them in terms of religion, occupation, family life, values? What do you intuit to be their challenges, joys, and sorrows? Take time to notice their expressions, pace, companions, etc. Open to their lives, not assuming that you know what is good for them. Prayerfully ask God how best to respond to the persons in your immediate environment.

At the very least, you can bless the people that you meet, noticing the "ordinary" people in your life (store clerks, toll booth operators, receptionists, co-workers), and blessing them, and placing them in God's care.

When we are connected to God, we are connected to others. When we are connected to others, we are connected to God. In the spirit of Paul's affirmation: "in God we live and move and have our being," experience God in every breath and in everything you see. Experience the events and encounters of your life as windows into God's presence. Experience your connection with God in everything and everyone.

Transforming Affirmations.

Spiritual affirmations are ways that we connect to the deeper realities of life. In repeating spiritual affirmations, we reframe our lives and renew our minds. We are no longer conformed to false limitations, but are "transformed by the renewing of our minds." Spiritual affirmations heal both the conscious and unconscious minds, and open us to divine insight, energy, and inspiration.

In this chapter, we will focus on three affirmations emerging from Acts 17. Repeat them several times each day, especially when you feel yourself being trapped by unhealthy behaviors or limitations.

> *God is the reality in whom I live and move and have my being.*
> *God is near me at all times.*
> *I am God's child. I am God's offspring.*
> *I treat everyone as God's beloved child.*

Manifesting Mission.

Mission takes many forms, some are primarily theological and evangelistic, while others involve social concern and justice. Today, we know that our mission is, first of all, where we live and not some far off place. Being faithful to the Way of Jesus involves walking the talk and talking the walk. What we believe shapes our behavior, but our beliefs are made flesh in everyday life. The love of God is not just a theological doctrine, but the inspiration to a life of reconciliation and healing. Believing that God speaks through young and old, male and female, slave and free, challenges us to honor and respect the rich diversity of human experience. Affirming that God is the reality in whom we live and move and have our being inspires us to become God's partners in healing the earth.

As a matter of personal reflection, consider the following: If someone were to ask you, "What are your deepest beliefs?" how would you respond? What beliefs or doctrines most shape your understanding of God, the world, humankind, the meaning of life, and the afterlife?

Acts of the Apostles is clear that doctrines are symbiotically related to behavior. Our doctrines emerge from spirit-centered experiences. Our experiences are clarified by our beliefs and take shape in practical application. Accordingly, what behaviors might your beliefs inspire in the areas of:

- » Personal stewardship
- » Care of family and children
- » Marriage and other significant relationships

» Community involvement
» Political involvement
» Care of the Earth
» Response to diverse opinions
» Ways we respond to personal or global conflict (violence, reconciliation, consensus, peace-seeking balanced by appropriate protection).
» Involvement in justice issues – first-hand support of vulnerable people and/or political involvement to achieve a social order more reflective of Jesus' values.

TWO

PRAYERFUL PREPARATION

So when they had come together, they asked him, "Lord, is this the time when you will restore the kingdom to Israel?" ⁷He replied, "It is not for you to know the times or periods that the Father has set by his own authority. ⁸But you will receive power when the Holy Spirit has come upon you; and you will be my witnesses in Jerusalem, in all Judea and Samaria, and to the ends of the earth." ⁹When he had said this, as they were watching, he was lifted up, and a cloud took him out of their sight. ¹⁰While he was going and they were gazing up towards heaven, suddenly two men in white robes stood by them. ¹¹They said, "Men of Galilee, why do you stand looking up towards heaven? This Jesus, who has been taken up from you into heaven, will come in the same way as you saw him go into heaven."

¹²Then they returned to Jerusalem from the mount called Olivet, which is near Jerusalem, a sabbath day's journey away. ¹³When they had entered the city, they went to the room upstairs where they were staying, Peter, and John, and James, and Andrew, Philip and Thomas, Bartholomew and Matthew, James son of Alphaeus, and Simon the Zealot, and Judas son of James. ¹⁴All these were constantly devoting themselves to prayer, together with certain women, including Mary the mother of Jesus, as well as his brothers.

[As they considered someone to take Judas' place, they came to the following conclusion, vv. 15-20] *"¹⁵⁻²¹So one of the men who have accompanied us throughout the time that the Lord Jesus went in and out among us, ²²beginning from the baptism of John until the day when he was taken up from us—one of these must become a witness with us to his resurrection." ²³So they proposed two, Joseph called Barsabbas,* *who was also known as Justus, and Matthias. ²⁴Then they prayed and said, "Lord, you know everyone's heart. Show us which one of these two you have chosen ²⁵to take the place in this ministry and apostleship from which Judas turned aside to go to his own place." ²⁶And they cast lots for them, and the lot fell on Matthias; and he was added to the eleven apostles.* (Acts 1:1-14, 21-26)

THIS IS THE DAY THAT GOD HAS MADE

Do you remember what happened on May 21, 2011 or October 21, 2011? Well, according to those who were awaiting the Second Coming of Jesus, "Absolutely nothing!"

Remember all the fuss about radio evangelist Harold Camping, who was absolutely sure that at 6:00 p.m. on May 21, 2011 Jesus would come again bringing both celebration and destruction. After the predicted rapture of the saints and destruction of the earth did not occur, he revised his prediction to October 21, 2011 and once again, life went on as usual, babies were born, people went to work, and believers were disappointed. Like countless others before him, Camping's prognostications failed despite his certainty and the ardor of his followers. Camping has since repudiated his attempt to discern the signs of the times as sinful and admits that he should have paid attention to those who challenged him to heed Jesus' warning: "But about that day and hour no one knows, not the angels in heaven, nor the Son, but only the Father" (Matthew 24:36).

Recently, a number of people – ad agencies and booksellers – have made a lot of money on their interpretations of the Mayan calendar. Some people predicted that the world would end on December 21, 2012, the final day of the 5,125th year of a cycle of years, according to Mayan calculations. The more optimistic among us hoped that December 21 would usher in a new age of spiritual awakening and convergence, the Age of Aquarius, when, as the song from the rock musical "Hair" proclaims, "Peace will guide the planets and love will steer the stars."

Needless to say, no Mayan scholars could find any evidence that the Mesoamerican tribe saw the end of the cycle as the end of the world! They may just have run out of space on the stone they were inscribing! As I pen these words in September 2012, I suspect that Christmas will come and go and life will continue on our complex, beautiful, ambiguous, and always surprising planet.

I suspect that in the wake of the resurrection, Jesus' disciples wanted to escape the challenges and ambiguities of the world. Hoping for an answer that would put an end to the suspense, they plead "When will you restore the realm of God to Israel?" Jesus' response is clear and unambiguous and it echoes through the ages challenging any premature attempt to escape our worldly responsibilities: "It is not for you to know the times or periods God has set by divine authority."

As we ponder God's role in bringing our planet's life to fulfillment, the issue is not divine predestination that eliminates human agency, but divine invitation that says, "This is the day brought forth by my loving wisdom. You are alive. I will be with you, shaping the movements of history, but this world is also in your hands. You have a role in shaping the present and future." In the meantime, "you will receive power when the Holy Spirit has come upon you." God gives us the vision, the agency, and the energy to respond creatively to whatever crises we face in our personal, congregational, and planetary lives.

What is this divine power? It is the power of the birth of the universe, still coursing through our cells and souls. It is the wisdom that shaped the upward movements of creation, described poetically in Genesis and scientifically in the theory of evolution, quantum physics, relativity theory, and the discovery of the Higgs Boson "god" particle. It is the strength and endurance to face the unavoidable and sometimes unexpected crises of life. It is the healing energy embodied in prayer and touch that transforms bodies, spirits, emotions, and relationships.

Our ultimate salvation is in God's loving hands, but we work it out day by day in this world. As Paul says in Philippians, "God is near." God's nearness and fidelity, Paul asserts, is the source of our joy as followers of Jesus (Philippians 4:4-9). If God is omnipresent, then this world is also heavenly and filled with grace and opportunity. Each moment contains within it the coming of Christ and the fullness of God's kingdom. We just need to play our part as spiritually aware companions of God and our fellow creatures.

As a theologian, I study the great words of faith, trying to convey what they mean and how we can understand them in our world. One of my favorite theological words is "omnipresence." Now, omnipresence is a word that is seldom taken seriously – because if we did believe it, everything would change. It means that God is everywhere. It means that God is here. It means that God is in my life and God is in your life. As the angelic figures in Isaiah's mystical experience in the temple proclaim, "the whole earth is filled with God's glory!" (See Isaiah's mystical experience, described in Isaiah 6:1-8.) If the whole earth is filled with God's glory, then God's glory fills you, whether or not you are currently aware of it!

"Omnipresence" is still an important word for us. It tells us that wherever we are, God is present; and that "nothing can separate us from the love of God" (Romans 8:38-39). It tells us that we don't have to go to heaven to find God – God is right here and our task is to make this world as heavenly as possible. As the Lord's Prayer proclaims, "thy kingdom come, thy will be done, on earth as it is in heaven" (Matthew 6:9-13)!

Don't Look Up, Look Around

Now, I recall hearing a sermon – and you hear a lot of interesting sermons if you're a theologian – in which the preacher proclaimed that if we got into a rocket ship and left the earth's atmosphere, we would eventually arrive at a geographical place called heaven. He might have gained credence for his belief from the account of Jesus' ascension into the heavens. As the story goes, Jesus gives a final message to his followers, and then off he goes – floating up to heaven. At the very least, Jesus' ascension is challenging to 21st century people: it defies our understanding of the universe. But, to Luke, the ascension of Jesus serves an important theological purpose: Jesus is now offstage – away from the action – and like the parent of young adults who have just gone away to college, placing responsibility in her or his children's hands.

I don't wish to question Luke, the presumed author of Acts, but few people today believe we live in a three story universe envisioned by first-century followers of Jesus – heaven above, the underworld beneath, and earth at the center. We live in a de-centered universe, by all accounts at least 13.7 billion years of age and containing approximately 125 billion galaxies, each with at least a billion solar systems like ours, which is a fancy way that cosmologists – people who study the universe's origins and extent – admit that the universe is grander and more immense than anyone can imagine!

Now, in every religious tradition, there are a lot of people who are "so heavenly minded that they are no earthly good." They see this lifetime as the front porch to eternity, investing all their energy in the afterlife, in saving their souls, and forgetting that this world, the one we live in, is in need of healing and salvation, too! In fact, Jesus' followers are told to look around, perceptively and prayerfully, to find their mission here and not in some celestial plane.

Jesus has just told his disciples that faith involves living in the present, embracing the beauty and our responsibility in the present moment. As the disciples gaze longingly at the skies perhaps hoping to be drawn up to heaven, angelic figures continue Jesus' lesson in theology and ethics: your work is not only in the present moment, as Jesus told you; but, your faithfulness to Jesus' cause is embodied right where you are. "What are you doing looking at the heavens?" they challenge.

We are embodied, social beings, arising from a long evolutionary journey that joins us with all creation. Our callings – and each of us has many callings that emerge over time and in various contexts – in life happen in the concrete settings of our lives, amid the complexity of politics, family life, health and illness, civic responsibility, and planetary citizenship. Turning away from this earth – hoping for divine rescue and earthy destruction – is treason to God's vision for us and our world. Loving God is always connected with loving and honoring creation in all its variety and temporality. The grass will be gone tomorrow, as Jesus advices, but it is sure beautiful today!

As spiritual teacher Gerald May proclaims, spiritual practice involves *pausing, noticing, opening, stretching* and *yielding,* and *responding* to this very moment of beauty, wonder, and adventure. Elizabeth Barrett Browning captures the creation-affirming spirituality of Acts in the language of poetry:

> Earth's crammed with heaven,
> And every common bush afire with God;
> But only he [or she] who sees, takes off his shoes –
> The rest sit round it and pluck blackberries.

There's nothing wrong with blackberries, by the way, but encountering God makes the everyday events of life holy and challenges us to bring beauty and love to the universe.

Don't Do Something, Wait Prayerfully

In the wake of the ascension, the apostles return to their meeting place and, for the next several days, constantly devote themselves to prayer. We don't know the nature of their individual prayer practices. They may have been a blend of quiet contemplation, praise, intercession, celebration of Jesus' last supper, and thanksgiving. But prayer was their priority as a community before they undertook any action. They knew that God's power was coming, and also knew that power without prayer is destructive to us and others.

At a recent congregational meeting I attended, one of the church leaders raised the question, "Have we prayed about this course of action?" His question was revealing and evoked a variety of responses from his fellow board members. People shared the depth of their concern and their willingness to look for a greater perspective than their own. In ways that don't always happen in church meetings, the members revealed their prayer lives, witnessing to the fact that there are a variety of prayer forms, appropriate to individuals' and communities' personalities and values. Some board members confessed that although they didn't pray often, they had "looked for wisdom" in relationship to the decision at hand. Others noted that they looked to scripture for guidance. Still others retreated to a quiet place for contemplation before advocating a certain course of action. The board members recognized that although prayer does not always insure personal success or congregational numerical growth, prayer connects us with a deeper wisdom and helps us identify resources and strategies to promote God's mission in our world.

TIME TO ACT

The apostles have a decision to make. Prayerful discernment prepared the community for wise action. With the departure of Judas, they need one more member on the spiritual leadership team. So they do something curious by our contemporary thinking, they cast lots. Today we might draw cards, play "paper, scissors, rock," randomly choose the short stick or a marked piece of paper, or look for insight by consulting the *I Ching* or a Tarot card reader. Sounds like a strange way to choose a leader, doesn't it!

But, the community is not depending on mere chance. They trust God's guidance moving through their community. What they are depending on is the presence of divine wisdom – what the psychiatrist Carl Jung called synchronicity – working not only within the process of casting lots but also in every step of the decision-making process beginning with their prayerful community retreat. Synchronicity is the meaningful coincidence that lies beneath what appears to be random and unplanned. If we believe that God is omnipresent – present everywhere and in everything – and also omni-active – providing possibilities and energy for abundant living in every situation – then each moment, to a greater or lesser degree, reflects God's wisdom. When we take time to open ourselves to God's greater wisdom, we can intuit God's vision for our lives.

Our vocations – our callings and gifts and talents – and how we use them moment by moment are not fixed or determined but emerge in every situation and encounter. Every moment of our lives joins the impact of the past and our environment and the lure of larger, divine purposes that take us toward the future and beyond our self-interest – and God is present in these details of our lives. In the prayerful interplay of divine call and human response, apparently random acts such as casting lots reflect a deeper wisdom that can guide us in making personal and corporate decisions. This "higher creativity" joins quiet withdrawal with decisive action: prayerful gestation gives birth to wise and world-changing action.

WHAT ABOUT BARSABBAS?

I can identify with Joseph, also known as Barsabbas and Justus, who was put up as a candidate for the inner circle of leaders, but passed over. I wonder if he was disappointed or relieved when Matthias' name came up as Judas' successor. I wonder if he asked himself, "Why wasn't I chosen? Didn't God think I was good enough to be an apostle?" This morning, as I was preparing to reflect on this passage, I received an e-mail informing me that I was not the first choice for a pastoral position for which I interviewed. I truly hoped I'd be called to this congregation and believed that I would enable them to grow spiritually and numerically in the years ahead. For a few minutes, I felt both disappointment and angst. I wondered if at nearly sixty, despite my previous successes, gifts, and diverse experiences, I would ever secure another full-time congregational or seminary position. It is realistic to ask such questions and healthy to allow feelings of disappointment surface. Still, within the limitations of life, there is a deeper realism that guides our steps toward new possibilities even when our path takes us through the valley of failure.

At such moments of apparent failure, I take comfort as well as inspiration in recognizing that there is a gentle providence that runs through our lives, providing us new possibilities when certain pathways close. As the Quakers have long counseled, a way will be made even when it appears there is no way ahead. Faithfulness always contains a strong sense of agnosticism, the recognition that we never fully have all the answers, see the big picture of our lives, or know what's best for us and others. This creative humility gives us the courage to continue – and the ability to let go of yesterday's hopes and failures – when what we counted on doesn't come to pass. God is a fountain of possibility: the limitations of life, the concreteness of success and failure, the womb from which new adventures emerge. Perhaps, Barsabbas took solace not only in the fact that Matthias' gifts were right for spiritual leadership, but also that his own gifts inclined him toward another type of ministry.

The unsuccessful candidate, Justus Barsabbas disappears from the biblical narrative as quickly as he appears. According to some legends, despite his apparent failure at apostleship, Barsabbas became Bishop of Eleutheropolis, where he died at the hand of persecutors as a witness for Christ. While he might not have made it to the inner circle, his faithful following of God's vision still shapes the Jesus movement today.

TRANSFORMING ACTS

Opening to the Spirit.

My friend and colleague Patricia Adams Farmer speaks of the importance of taking a regular "beauty break" to awaken our senses and spirits to the wonders of life. There is no particular methodology, simply find a place that nurtures your spirit: your backyard, a park, a hiking trail, the seashore, or simply your neighborhood. Then, spend at least ten minutes, sitting or walking, noticing the beauty in your environment. Make it a point to take time off for a few minutes each day to bathe your senses in beauty, whether among humans, nature, or non-human animals.

In the spirit of the beauty break, this exercise focuses on seeing the divine in every encounter. You might begin by listening to Carrie Newcomer's "Holy as a Day is Spent" in which the singer-songwriter describes the wonder of simple things like frying eggs, folding laundry, watching a dog run in her sleep, busy streets, check out girls, and the changing seasons. Open your eyes to see deeply into every person, perhaps by prompting yourself with words like "I see God in you" or "You are God's beloved child." Take time to pay attention to service people, housekeeping staff, and others we often overlook. Find ways to contribute something of beauty and goodness in every encounter, for the world is saved one person and moment at a time.

Transforming Affirmations.

Affirmations ground us in the here and now. They transform our perception and, accordingly, transform the world we experience. Enemies can become friends. Polarizing viewpoints can be transformed into aesthetic contrasts and, in politics, red and blue can become purple.

In the days ahead, repeat throughout the day the following affirmations:

> *I walk with beauty all around me. I see beauty everywhere.*
> *This is God's world. I bring beauty and healing to the Earth.*
> *I see holiness in everyone I meet.*

Manifesting Mission.

Contemporary theology has expanded our understanding of salvation to embrace this lifetime – healing and wholeness –as well as the afterlife. We are called to be God's partners in healing the Earth.

To any open-minded observer, the Earth is in trouble. Virtually every reputable study recognizes the impact of human actions in global climate change. While we cannot do everything, we can do meaningful things to promote planetary well-being. As the angelic figures assert, don't look up, look around you. You'll find your mission right here.

Let the following questions serve as an examination of conscience which may lead to changed behaviors:

» Do you regularly recycle?
» Do you walk (if physically able) distances of less than a mile rather than drive an automobile?
» If it is available and not burdensome, do you take public transportation to work, recreational activities, and friend's homes?
» Do you monitor your home energy consumption – heating, cooling, lights, appliances, etc.?
» Do you see a relationship between consumption, auto mileage, and the pollution of the environment?
» Are there creative, non-polarizing, ways that you as a Christian can bring attention to the environmental crisis in your congregation, neighborhood, and among political decision-makers?

THREE

SPIRIT-CENTERED FAITH

When the day of Pentecost had come, they were all together in one place. ²And suddenly from heaven there came a sound like the rush of a violent wind, and it filled the entire house where they were sitting. ³Divided tongues, as of fire, appeared among them, and a tongue rested on each of them. ⁴All of them were filled with the Holy Spirit and began to speak in other languages, as the Spirit gave them ability.

⁵Now there were devout Jews from every nation under heaven living in Jerusalem. ⁶And at this sound the crowd gathered and was bewildered, because each one heard them speaking in the native language of each. ⁷Amazed and astonished, they asked, "Are not all these who are speaking Galileans? ⁸And how is it that we hear, each of us, in our own native language? ⁹Parthians, Medes, Elamites, and residents of Mesopotamia, Judea and Cappadocia, Pontus and Asia, ¹⁰Phrygia and Pamphylia, Egypt and the parts of Libya belonging to Cyrene, and visitors from Rome, both Jews and proselytes, ¹¹Cretans and Arabs—in our own languages we hear them speaking about God's deeds of power." ¹²All were amazed and perplexed, saying to one another, "What does this mean?" ¹³But others sneered and said, "They are filled with new wine."

¹⁴But Peter, standing with the eleven, raised his voice and addressed them, "Men of Judea and all who live in Jerusalem, let this be known to you, and listen to what I say. ¹⁵Indeed, these are not drunk, as you suppose, for it is only nine o'clock in the morning. ¹⁶No, this is what was spoken through the prophet Joel: ¹⁷'In the last days it will be, God declares, that I will pour out my Spirit upon all flesh, and your sons and your daughters shall prophesy, and your young men shall see visions, and your old men shall dream dreams. ¹⁸Even upon my slaves, both men and women, in those days I will pour out my Spirit; and *they shall prophesy. *[19]*And I will show portents in the heaven above and signs on the earth below, blood, and fire, and smoky mist. *[20]*The sun shall be turned to darkness and the moon to blood, before the coming of the Lord's great and glorious day. *[21]*Then everyone who calls on the name of the Lord shall be saved." *(Acts 2:1-21)

SEISMIC SPIRITUALITY

Author Annie Dillard counsels that whenever we go to church, we should expect great surprises, that shake us up and leave us forever changed. The author believes that we expect too little from God and in consequence too little from ourselves in our worship and mission to the world. At church, we make great requests and speak about things that should both comfort and terrify us. In Dillard's words:

> On the whole, I do not find Christians, outside of the catacombs, sufficiently sensible of conditions. Does anyone have the foggiest idea what sort of power we so blithely invoke? Or, as I suspect, does no one believe a word of it? The churches are children playing on the floor with their chemistry sets, mixing up a batch of TNT to kill a Sunday morning. It is madness to wear ladies' straw hats and velvet hats to church; we should all be wearing crash helmets. Ushers should issue life preservers and signal flares; they should lash us to our pews. For the sleeping god may wake someday and take offense, or the waking god may draw us out to where we can never return.[1]

As C.S. Lewis remarks in *The Lion, The Witch, and the Wardrobe,* the God we worship is a lion who is never entirely tame or safe, despite God's passionate love for us.

Think for a moment: If suddenly, a mighty wind blew through your sanctuary and flames burned brightly above each head and a few of us took to our feet and started dancing and chanting in strange tongues, what would your response be? Would you join

---

1 Annie Dillard, *Teaching a Stone to Talk* (New York: Harper and Row, 1982), p. 40.

in? Run for cover? Would you embrace the chaos? Or, vow never
to return?

While words can never fully describe any experience – especially the most important ones like falling in love, sitting
at the bedside in the final hours of a beloved friend or parent,
or feeling God's presence surrounding and filling us – when
I asked this question of a doctoral class at Wesley Theological Seminary, my students responded with words such as:
"I'd dive under the pews!" "I'd run for cover!" "I'd sprint out the
door!" "I'd start shouting, too!" and "I'd let the wind take me away!"

I am sure the first Pentecost community was surprised and
amazed as well. Though they prayed for the coming of the Spirit,
they had no idea what to expect. But, on that day during the feast
of Pentecost, they received what they were promised and experienced the answer to their prayers, which surely was more than they
had imagined. God's power can be awesome and the flames of the
spirit can burn as well as warm. Still, somehow, as shaken and overwhelmed as they were, they rallied and went with the flow – their
encounter with God drove them into the streets where they began
to preach, speaking God's good news in ways that everyone could
understand despite differences in language and ethnicity. Their
mystical experiences led to mission and to creating ever-widening
circles of hospitality and grace.

A COMMUNITY OF MYSTICS

Many evangelicals are suspicious of the mysticism. They believe that a direct encounter with the Holy One may draw us away
from the witness of God in Jesus Christ and Holy Scripture. Many
liberals are equally suspicious of mystical experiences. They think
that mysticism draws us away from social concern and our responsibility to heal this world. Moreover, many liberals are uneasy with
anything that seems to go beyond reason or reveal unexpected
bursts of divine energy or inspiration. They fear supernatural in-
terventions that upset the regularity of cause and effect.

The Pentecostal experience was first and foremost communal. It was also concrete and contextual. Perhaps, the Spirit's sighs too deep for words, ever-operative deep within us, burst forth not as an external, supernatural event, but the fullest expression of God's presence in this particular moment. The Spirit's movements did not come unbidden and without context, but were intimately connected with the prayers of Jesus' followers. Their prayers opened the windows for wind and fire to transform their spirits.

Can you imagine the catalytic effect of a community that takes prayer seriously? God's Spirit is present everywhere in human and non-human life. But, the Spirit makes herself known most fully when we make a home for her by our prayers, community life, and mission? Like Wisdom/Sophia, described in Proverbs, God's Spirit calls at the marketplace and street corner, "Listen, follow me, open to my adventurous mission, and you will find a vocation that brings peace, meaning, and also excitement!"

SPIRIT OF UNITY – SPIRIT OF DIVERSITY

On that day, Jerusalem hosted Jewish worshipers from throughout the known world. They had come for the Pentecost festival, traveling great distances at great sacrifice to deepen their faith and give glory to the God of Israel. No doubt they expected meaningful prayer and worship, but few expected to be part of a spiritual earthquake. Luke describes the ethnic diversity of the Pentecost pilgrims and their surprise at the words of the Apostles: "And how is it that we hear, each of us, in our own native language? [9]Parthians, Medes, Elamites, and residents of Mesopotamia, Judea and Cappadocia, Pontus and Asia, [10]Phrygia and Pamphylia, Egypt and the parts of Libya belonging to Cyrene, and visitors from Rome, both Jews and proselytes, [11]Cretans and Arabs–in our own languages we hear them speaking about God's deeds of power" (Acts 2:8-11).

Divine inspiration transcends and transforms diversity. Everyone hears in her or his own language. They united in their active participation in the movements of God's spirit. Though some scoffed at this astounding revelation of divine unity, the Spirit continues to move, uniting the separated and creating a new community of faith.

United as they are, this community also honored diversity. Medes were not asked to become like Elamites and Parthians were not asked to follow the cultural practices of Pamphylians, nor was anyone asked to become a cultural Jew. The Pentecost spirit created a unity in Christ that embraced and affirmed diversity.

Pentecost reflects God's own quest to balance unity and diversity. God loves diversity. Just look at the non-human world in its wondrous variety. Explore the many hues of humankind and the many gifts of culture. Pentecost faith challenges us to affirm two important things: God's Spirit makes us one and God's Spirit brings out the gifts of our diversity. Today, the movements of the Spirit are inspiring many new forms of Christianity alongside traditional Eastern and Western Christianity. We can rejoice in the imagination and innovations of emerging Christianity, the growing Pentecostal movement in the Southern hemisphere, the rebirth of socially conscious evangelical Christianity, and the revival of open-spirited progressive Christian faith. Like the colors on a palette, we recognize differences, but difference calls us to affirm contrast rather than opposition even when we challenge one another's theological, social, or ethical positions. One in the Spirit, we delight in our manifold diversity.

A DEMOCRACY OF THE SPIRIT

Just as surprised as anyone else, I suspect, the apostle Peter finally composed himself and led by the Spirit recalled words from the prophet Joel:

> *I will pour my Spirit upon all flesh,*
> *And your sons and daughters shall prophesy,*
> *And your young men shall see visions,*
> *And your old men shall dream dreams.*
> *Even upon my slaves, both women and men,*

In those days, I will pour out my Spirit
And they shall prophesy....
Everyone who calls upon the name of God will be saved.
(Joel 2:28-32)

Everyone gets a piece of revelation – all the barriers of race, age, economics, gender, and – dare we say – sexual orientation (given Philip's encounter with the Ethiopian eunuch) are broken down. No one is left behind or denied the ability to experience God's presence and find wholeness now and forevermore.

Inspired by God, Peter proclaims a democracy of the Spirit that builds on Joel's vision of Shalom. Saying more than he can imagine and challenging his own parochial prejudices, Peter is driven to affirm that God's love embraces all creation and every race. For a while, this will be purely theoretical for Peter, but when Cornelius' servants knock on his door, his ideals will become a reality. He will have walk the talk of inclusion and let go of any ethnic superiority or separatism.

Can you imagine a democracy of the spirit? Can you awaken to God's voice speaking through infants and toddlers, recovering substance abusers and the GLBT community, wealthy business people and community organizers, welfare mothers and soccer moms? God's Spirit moves everywhere and any and everyone can be a vehicle of God's word to us. Recipients of the Spirit's insight even include non-Christians, as the stories of the magi and the king of Nineveh reveal. Don't stand in the way of revelation! A little child can lead us and so can a foreigner!

Now, we don't need dramatic religious experiences to have Pentecost encounters: we simply need to open our eyes to the insight, inspiration, and wonder within us and all around us. We need to allow our spirits to be stretched to the point that no one is a stranger, no one is left out, and no one is denied full access to our care or God's love. There is no polarization, no second class citizenship, no outsider status – in those moments, we experience our own kind of Pentecost and the hint of God's intention for all of creation.

WHEN MYSTICISM BECOMES MISSION

Pentecost proclaims that God's wisdom is available to all of us. Everyone can be transformed and experience new life. In some circles, spirituality and mission are in tension. Some conservative Christians see spirituality as preparing us for the afterlife. We don't need to involve ourselves in social justice issues. Kindness to neighbor suffices as we train our eyes on eternity. Just a closer walk with God is all we need to fulfill our vocation as Christians. Some humorously describe such Christians as so heavenly minded that they are no earthly good!

On the other hand, some liberal Christians emphasize social action to the extent that prayer and meditation are seen as superfluous distractions from the real problems of our time. Constantly busy with good works, many activists burn out and become cynical at the slow arc of social transformation. Holistic faith involves both action and contemplation and that's the heart of the Pentecost message. Mystical experiences by themselves become irrelevant. "If I speak in the tongues of mortals and of angels, but do not have love, I am a noisy gong or a clanging cymbal." Social action without spirituality depletes the spirit and leads to disillusionment. "If I give away all my possessions ... but have not love, I am nothing" (I Corinthians 13:1, 3).

On Pentecost mysticism inspired mission. Jesus' first followers were driven by the Spirit into the streets to share good news that leads to everlasting life. They let the fires of the Spirit warm and the winds of the Spirit challenge their community. Prayerfulness led to passion for changing the world.

PRACTICING PENTECOST

This amazing coming of God's Spirit invites us to "practice Pentecost" in our everyday lives. Now, grace happens without us seeking it, and once in a while we encounter a light on the road to Damascus like the apostle Paul, but most of the time, we need to practice what we are seeking. We need to prepare ourselves with

prayer and community. Here are a few Pentecost practices that open
the door to greater manifestations of the Spirit:

First, surround yourself with people who believe surprising
things can happen to you and the world. At church we should
expect great things of ourselves and great things of God and this
community. Limited and prone to self-interest, we can still do
ordinary things, as Mother Theresa says, in extraordinary ways.
What great thing is God calling you toward? What great thing lies
ahead for your congregation?

Second, open yourself to new insights. A living faith is always
growing. Familiar scriptures can come alive in new ways if we risk
challenging old assumptions. Outmoded doctrines can give birth
to deeper understandings of God and the world if we take time to
ask questions and prayerfully embrace innovative visions. What
new idea and inspiration is on the horizon for you and this church?

Third, widen your circle of compassion and care. Peter proclaims a democracy of the Spirit that reflects God's care for all
people, without exception. Claiming this universalism was difficult
for the early church. It took time for their theological insights
to take shape in radical hospitality. But, they did the hard work
of challenging preconceived boundaries of grace to be faithful to
God's unhindered gospel. As you look at your life and the life of
your congregation: Is anyone left out? Do we deny full humanity to
anyone? Do we see certain people as unworthy of God's care? Take
time to challenge your limits of love, embrace, and inclusion. As
Mother Theresa said of the dying street people of Calcutta, India,
"Here I see God in all of God's distressing disguises." Deep down
Jesus comes to us in every face and every encounter. Acts reminds
us that we want to be ready to greet Christ wherever he shows up
in our lives.

Finally, we can listen to the Spirit's voice in our sighs too
deep for words, in our dreams, insights, hunches, and unexpected
moments of insight, and in the words of small children who, if we
listen to them, might awaken us to the wonders of life and the lost
joy of our own childhoods.

While you may not need to strap on a safety belt, put on a life vest, or put on a crash helmet next time you come to church, you can sing "Hallelujah" and other great things in worship. You can listen for God's voice in small children and barking dogs, reach out beyond your comfort zone, and speak the good news of welcome to everyone.

TRANSFORMING ACTS

Opening to Pentecost.

Wind and fire are central to the Pentecost experience. God breathed on them and filled them with light. In this exercise, take a moment to relax, breathing calmly and regularly. Then, more mindfully visualize God's Spirit filling you with every breath, bringing health and vitality. After a few minutes, begin to visualize a holy light entering you with every breath. Experience it filling your whole being from head to toe and then surrounding you in a protective but flexible shield from all danger. You are strong and safe in God's care. Finally, begin to imagine your exhaling as sending God's light into the world to heal and transform anyone it touches. Close after a period of ten to fifteen minutes with a prayer of thanksgiving for God's loving light and healing breath and your role in sharing God's light with the world. God is always inspiring us and every breath can be a prayer.

Transforming Affirmations.

Using spiritual affirmations is a simple way to practice Pentecost. Repeating positive words awakens us to God's presence and enables us to more fully experience God's vision for our lives and embrace God's energy of creative transformation. In line with the Pentecost experience, try practicing these affirmations throughout the day:

God's Spirit enlivens me with every breath.
God's Spirit inspires me to mission.
Every breath I take is a prayer of blessing.

Manifesting Mission.

Our prayers join head, hands, and heart. In the spirit of Pentecost, we are called to go out into the world sharing good news – news of healing, grace, love, and transformation. Consider the following:

> » Where is God leading you in terms of mission in your community?
> » Where is God calling you to help advance your congregation's mission in the larger community?
> » In what ways can you embody God's good news in everyday life?
> » Where is your congregation being called to minister to the needs of your community?

Throughout the day, take time to pause and notice places where you can share good news with others. In response to your openness to ordinary mission, reach out in ways that bless and heal others. For example, you can ask if your assistance is needed to help someone carrying a heavy load or looking lost. You can specifically say "thank you" to service workers, postal carriers, checkout clerks, and others who we often don't notice in our busy schedules. In what ways might you respond today to a pressing social concern – explore volunteering, call you representative about a public policy issue, make a donation to a cause that supports vulnerable persons or care for the Earth. Every positive action radiates across the Earth, creating the possibility of planetary healing and peace among the nations.

FOUR

GLORY, GRATITUDE, AND GENEROSITY

They devoted themselves to the apostles' teaching and fellowship, to the breaking of bread and the prayers. [43]Awe came upon everyone, because many wonders and signs were being done by the apostles. [44]All who believed were together and had all things in common; [45]they would sell their possessions and goods and distribute the proceeds to all, as any had need. [46]Day by day, as they spent much time together in the temple, they broke bread at home and ate their food with glad and generous hearts, [47]praising God and having the goodwill of all the people. And day by day the Lord added to their number those who were being saved. (Acts 2:42-47)

Now the whole group of those who believed were of one heart and soul, and no one claimed private ownership of any possessions, but everything they owned was held in common. [33]With great power the apostles gave their testimony to the resurrection of the Lord Jesus, and great grace was upon them all. [34]There was not a needy person among them, for as many as owned lands or houses sold them and brought the proceeds of what was sold. [35]They laid it at the apostles' feet, and it was distributed to each as any had need. [36]There was a Levite, a native of Cyprus, Joseph, to whom the apostles gave the name Barnabas (which means "son of encouragement"). [37]He sold a field that belonged to him, then brought the money, and laid it at the apostles' feet. (Acts 4:32-37)

PRACTICAL THEOLOGY

A good friend of mine had an interesting pastoral challenge. As you may know, most church camp registration forms have questions regarding responsibility for the camper's health insurance. As my friend, a Disciples of Christ pastor, was reviewing camp registrations for the summer, he noticed that the space regarding health insurance was left blank on one registration form. He knew the child's family was among the working poor, that is, those who make enough money to get by, but not enough to qualify for government support or to purchase health insurance. After ruminating a bit, he took a bold step: he called the congregation's board of directors and following a time of prayer and discussion, they authorized him to place the congregation's name in the empty space, guaranteeing that the congregation would cover any health care expenses incurred during camp.

I suspect the actions of the early church were motivated by similar concerns: some new Christians came from wealthy families, others were tradesmen and women, still others were unemployed and disowned by their families as a result of following Jesus. Caught up in the universalism and ecstatic experiences of Pentecost, in which the wellsprings of salvation were opened to all people – old and young, slave and free, stranger and friend – they were forced to come to grips with financial inequalities existing in their own community. No doubt the leaders asked themselves: How can we claim to be one in the spirit if some of our members lack housing, food, and employment? How can we see ourselves as brothers and sisters in Christ if some are destitute while others flourish? We need to practice what we are preaching even if this means sacrifice on our part.

They did something unheard of in the Roman Empire: they shared their treasure with people outside their family and sold their possessions to support persons in need. They saw their personal property and comfort as subordinate to the well-being of others and recognized that the welfare of their neighbors was more compelling than their own financial security. As Paul says in his famous passage on the body of Christ, "when one suffers, all suffer; when one rejoices, all rejoice" (1 Corinthians 12:26, author's paraphrase).

It has been said that there are two radically different ways of looking at the world: through the eyes of abundance and the lens of scarcity. The early Christians discovered that their well-being, spiritual growth, and sense of God's presence were related to the well-being of their Christian brothers and sisters. Like Isaiah, who encountered God in the Temple, they realized that spirituality and action, faith and mission, and personal and community well-being were two sides of the same coin. Their self-interest expanded beyond their immediate family to embrace the whole community and then over time the Empire.

Today we hear a lot about practical theology, the interplay of belief and behavior in the lives of persons and institutions. The philosopher Alfred North Whitehead asserted that in the long run, a person's character and conduct depend on her or his deepest convictions. At Pentecost, ecstatic experience led to profound beliefs about the nature of reality:

» God is generous and graceful.
» God seeks unity of humankind.
» God affirms the importance of diversity.
» Salvation and grace are open to everyone.
» Jesus' sacrifice on the Cross transforms human life and enables us to experience unity with God.

For these first Christians, these statements were not abstract theological doctrines unrelated to daily life. They were intimately related to emerging theological affirmations that transformed their value systems, economic life, and attitudes toward property and possession.

» God's graceful generosity inspires our generosity.
» God's quest for unity challenges us to be one body, sharing the fruits of our labors.
» God's affirmation of diversity invites us to cross boundaries and treat diverse groups equitably.

» God's universal grace inspires hospitality to everyone.
» Jesus' sacrificial life calls us to sacrifice on behalf of one another and for the good of the community.

Theology is meant to be lived. Ecstasy leads to equality of opportunity. Mystical experiences inspire mission to vulnerable persons in the community and beyond.

HOLISTIC SPIRITUALITY

As Acts 2 proclaims that the first Christians "devoted themselves to the Apostles teaching, to the community, to shared meals, and to prayers .... All who believed were together and had all things in common; they would sell their possessions and goods and distribute the proceeds to all, as any had need." They did not separate economics from theology or spirituality. Within the body of Christ, unity of spirit leads to the quest for physical well-being. While there may have been inequalities in income and property, there was no destitution or neglect. Everyone had enough of the Earth's bounty to have the energy and inspiration to share the good news of God's life-transforming Shalom. Putting God first lead Jesus' first followers to generosity and sacrificial living in which the neighbor's need outweighed property rights and personal comfort.

While we may not be called, given our economic circumstances or family responsibilities, to such radical generosity, Acts 2 challenges us to go beyond feelings of greed and scarcity to recognize that our abundance is a gift from God, and that our resources are intended to bring well-being to others as well as security and happiness to ourselves. There is no us and them or me and mine in the realm of God. The person most pitied in biblical spirituality is the self-made person, Ayn Rand's rugged individualist, who asks nothing of others and sees generosity to the vulnerable persons as a sign of weakness. Spiritually inspired by the vision of the body of Christ, the early Christians recognized the profound interdependence of life. No one ever succeeds on their own, whether in spirituality, business, education, government, or personal life. Our successes emerge from a dynamic interplay of our own personal initiative, creativity, and responsibility and the efforts of others, whose sacrifices paved the way for our achievements.

Often we live by scarcity, when there are resources all around. We believe that we must insure our own security regardless of its impact on others. A friend of mine, who spent four decades advising churches on capital campaigns and stewardship programs, relates his approach to congregational finances. When he begins to work with a congregation, he often asks, "What are your resources?" The appropriate and typical response involves the value of property, endowment, savings, and budget and debit. Good common sense, if you ask me. Then my friend challenges their responses, "That's not what I asked! What are your congregation's total resources? What is the combined time, talent, and treasure of the whole congregation, that is, everyone, not just the church's assets?" My friend does not counsel people to cash in their stocks and retirement plans; but he challenges churches to see beyond their scarcity and discover that despite their current financial situation, they have greater resources than they had previously imagined. In fact, most average size congregations have millions of dollars of assets based on this calculation. My friend reminds us that how we use our money is often a matter of choice and values. He also notes that we have more than we think and that we should take seriously the mission of the church and the needs of members even if it means a shorter vacation or postponing an unnecessary purchase.

Spirituality involves head, heart, and hands. Gratitude and generosity was at the heart of the early church. Gratitude is the virtue of relationship. It recognizes that we are all here because of the efforts of others: physicians need patients, teachers need students, ministers need congregants, job creators need workers and consumers, and Christians need mentors and guides. We all stand in the need of grace and when we receive grace, we need to pass it on to others.

Meister Eckhardt, the German mystic, asserted that "if the only prayer you say is thank you, that will suffice." Thanksgiving roots us a in generous universe and liberates us from the prison of isolated individualism. As you consider your life, whose generosity and love help you get to this place in your spiritual journey? Who told you about Jesus? Who showed you what it meant to be faithful, or to become a person of character? Think a moment: was it a Sunday school teacher, a parent or grandparent, a pastor? Who helped you in your professional career: was it a mentor, a teacher, your first employer, a scholarship, or student loan? We cannot make it alone and we should not let the bounty of life end with ourselves. As the camp song proclaims, "pass it on."

A THINKING CHURCH

The first followers of Jesus "devoted themselves to the apostles' teaching and fellowship, to the breaking of bread and the prayers." They were a church whose spirituality was truly holistic. They prayed and they studied, and discovered study was a form of prayer. We need thinking Christians, who take theological reflection seriously, who ask serious questions, and challenge unhealthy and superficial images of God and human experience. As I write these words, a prominent preacher is asserting that the recent damage brought on New Orleans by Hurricane Isaac is God's punishment for the city's toleration of homosexuality. Years earlier, other preachers identified Katrina's devastation of New Orleans with divine retribution even though the French Quarter, the heart of GLBT activity, was spared. Still others identify earthquakes, AIDS, terrorist attacks, and cancer with God's will or recompense for sinful behavior. A thinking church, following in the footsteps of Job, Jonah, Amos, Jesus, Paul, Peter, and James challenges simplistic, self-serving, and harmful understandings of faith.

Good theological reflection, whether progressive or evangelical, is essential for the proclamation of God's good news in a pluralistic age. Study is not optional for pastors and spiritual leaders. A seminary colleague of mine shared a recent survey that indicated that the average pastor reads less than six books a year, and that not of all of these are theological, devotional, practical, or spiritual! Physicians and attorneys are required to continue their education throughout their careers. The same should be true of pastors and lay and ordained spiritual leaders. A thinking church, willing to address hard issues such as suffering, economic injustice, global climate change, and salvation requires leaders who cherish the interplay of study, prayer, and action. Today, more than ever, churches need thinking pastors who will challenge old ways and inspire new paths of Christian faithfulness.

The early church grew because it had a mission, reflecting its holistic understanding of faith: the first Christians experienced God as a personal reality, took time for study and worship, and considered generosity and gratitude central to its lifestyle. Today, we can let our light shine – we can ponder our financial values and priorities, we can take time to insure that everyone who enters the doors is greeted with hospitality, and that no one in our church goes hungry, is homeless, or lacks health care. We can look beyond our church to encourage public policies that promote the health and welfare not only of our people but of vulnerable persons across the Earth. This isn't politics – it doesn't favor liberals or conservatives, or Republicans or Democrats, but practical theology and spirituality, faith giving birth to loving action and recognition that all of God's children deserve welcome, love, and sustenance.

TRANSFORMING ACTS

Opening to the Spirit

One of my favorite lines from Dag Hammarksjold's *Markings* is:

For all that has been – thanks.
For all that shall be – yes!

The late Secretary General of the United Nations knew that gratitude opens up the future and creates a force field in which new and unexpected possibilities emerge. We need a vision of possibilities to face the challenges of global change, moving a sustainable economy while shifting to new forms of employment, sustaining and expanding health care, and responding spiritually to pluralism and mistrust of religious institutions.

In this exercise, simply say "thank you" to God and others for every gift along your pathway. This can be an inner exercise of noting our connections to others and their impact on our lives. It can also be a relational practice of expressing gratitude whenever we receive a benefit from others – past, present, or future. We can communicate our gratitude face to face, with an e-mail or text message, a Facebook wall posting or message, or a letter.

Throughout the day live gratefully and express gratitude in ways that bless and affirm others.

Transforming Affirmations

Affirmative spirituality opens hearts, minds, and hands. It creates new pathways neurologically and relationally. In response to the "beloved community" (Martin Luther King), described in Acts 2 and 4, repeat the following affirmations or variations in the course your day.

> *My God will supply all my needs* (Philippians 4:19).
> *God's abundance flows through my life to others.*
> *I have all the time, money, and energy I need to serve God and my neighbors.*

Manifesting Mission

Acts, chapters two and four, affirms the importance of individual sacrifice for the well-being of community. Our property is not entirely our own; it comes from God and is intended to be used for our well-being and the well-being of others. Acts suggests that in the body of Christ and beyond the poor have a moral claim on us to provide basic human needs and opportunities for success.

The ability to transcend self-interest is a matter of head, heart, and hands. Study is essential to personal and social transformation. In the spirit of Acts, Christian growth involves commitment to study as a form of prayer: scripture, devotional books, accessible theology, and texts on current issues in ethics, social concern, and ecology. You may also deepen your Christian maturity through on-line research, art, and devotional reading.

Manifesting mission involves a willingness to "live simply [and sacrificially] so others might live." What are the needs in your community? Who are the vulnerable persons in your congregation or neighborhood? What do you feel comfortable sharing to support their health and future success in terms of time, talent, and treasure? What might you need to sacrifice or defer to make a Christian commitment to the greater good?

FIVE

HEALING ACTS

One day Peter and John were going up to the temple at the hour of prayer, at three o'clock in the afternoon. ²And a man lame from birth was being carried in. People would lay him daily at the gate of the temple called the Beautiful Gate so that he could ask for alms from those entering the temple. ³When he saw Peter and John about to go into the temple, he asked them for alms. ⁴Peter looked intently at him, as did John, and said, "Look at us" ⁵And he fixed his attention on them, expecting to receive something from them. ⁶But Peter said, "I have no silver or gold, but what I have I give you; in the name of Jesus Christ of Nazareth, stand up and walk." ⁷And he took him by the right hand and raised him up; and immediately his feet and ankles were made strong. ⁸Jumping up, he stood and began to walk, and he entered the temple with them, walking and leaping and praising God. ⁹All the people saw him walking and praising God, ¹⁰and they recognized him as the one who used to sit and ask for alms at the Beautiful Gate of the temple; and they were filled with wonder and amazement at what had happened to him. (Acts 3:1-10)

Now many signs and wonders were done among the people through the apostles. And they were all together in Solomon's Portico. ¹³None of the rest dared to join them, but the people held them in high esteem. ¹⁴Yet more than ever believers were added to the Lord, great numbers of both men and women, ¹⁵so that they even carried out the sick into the streets, and laid them on cots and mats, in order that Peter's shadow might fall on some of them as he came by. ¹⁶A great number of people would also gather from the towns around Jerusalem, bringing the sick and those tormented by unclean spirits, and they were all cured. (Acts 5:12-16)

HEALING AND CURING

In my most recent congregation, two sayings greeted me whenever I entered the church building. A placard over the doorway to the social hall asserted. "Prayer changes things!" In the landing next to the pastor's study, a poster counseled each passerby: "God grant me the serenity to accept the things I cannot change; courage to change the things I can; and wisdom to know the difference." Both were sagely words for pastors and lay folk alike!

The interplay of prayer and healing has always been important to me. I grew up being confronted by the motto, "Prayer changes things," whenever I opened our refrigerator door, which was often, during my youth! I grew up in the 1950s, watching televangelist Kathryn Kuhlman, dressed in a diaphanous gown, and whispering softly "I believe in miracles," and seeing Oral Roberts slap people on the forehead and shouting, "Be healed." I grew up in an environment saturated by prayer – my mother was a devout Baptist and prayed for everything from headaches to car trips. My dad was a pastor, and I often accompanied him on his hospital visits, knowing that as I sat in the lobby, he would be praying at the bedside of a congregant.

As a child of a pastor, I overheard conversations about people "living on borrowed time," prayers for the faithful, and unanswered and answered prayers. Being prone to reflect on such things, I was troubled by the terrible things that happened to people in my small town just over the hill from Monterey, California. I ruminated long and hard about Bobby Thorpe, a boy in my fifth grade class, who – after a hunting trip with his father – died as the result of a loaded firearm going off as he pulled it from the family car. I couldn't understand why my Sunday school teacher was dying of cancer and a beloved church member was debilitated from diabetes and heart disease. We prayed regularly in our family and sometimes people got well, other times they didn't. From the perspective of my childhood piety, there was no rhyme or reason in terms of answered and unanswered prayer. I heard pious explanations: "It was God's will,"

"She's in a better place, at least her suffering is over," "Sometimes God's answer is 'yes,' other times 'no,' and still other times 'maybe.'" None of them seemed to satisfy my youthful questioning.

I believe that prayer makes a difference. I also believe that, despite medical studies, answers to prayer are still mysterious and involve many factors, not just our faith or God's intentionality and power. I have come to accept a distinction between "healing" and "curing," which does solve every problem, but puts prayer and healing in perspective. "Curing" involves the cessation of symptoms, the remission of cancer, recovery from a heart attack, broken bone, or sinus infection. "Healing" relates to our relationship to God and our sense of trust in God's love in every season of life. You can be cured without being healed if you still live by fear or return to habits that created the health crisis to begin with. You can be healed when a cure is not possible if you trust that nothing – not even death, diminishment, loss of memory, or chronic illness can separate you from the love of God.

Signs, Wonders, and Acts of Power

Jesus' first followers expected "signs and wonders." They believed that Jesus' healing energy was alive and well and operative among the followers of Jesus' way. They had experienced Jesus the healer – whose healing heart and hands – embraced outcasts and unclean persons, welcoming them into God's realm, transforming their spirits and often transforming their bodies. They remembered stories, and – in the case of the disciples and the earliest women followers – experienced acts of power in which divine energy flowed to a woman suffering from a gynecological ailment, in a healing touch or spittle that served as a cure for blindness, in a word of forgiveness that enabled a man to stand on his feet, and words that brought the distant healing of a foreigner's daughter.

Their teacher was a remarkable healer. He had no methodology; his compassion took many forms including touch and energy, awakening faith, words of exorcism, provocative questions, distant healing, hospitality and welcome, spittle and mud, and forgiveness. Jesus told his followers that they could do greater things. They could continue his ministry of hospitality, teaching, and healing.[1]

And, now in the weeks following Pentecost, the power of the Spirit gave them the energy and ability to raise spirits and heal bodies. Acts tells the story of a man healed by the invocation of the "name of Jesus." Peter calls upon Jesus' name and reaches out to this paralyzed man and the man rises up, jumping for joy and praising God for new life and new purpose.

I suspect that when the disciples called upon the name of Jesus, it was shorthand for what they experienced when they journeyed with the Healer and participated in his ministry of physical, spiritual, emotional, and relational transformation. I believe that they were claiming the energy of love that flowed through Jesus hands as their own vocation in response to vulnerable humanity. The first followers of Jesus were inspired by the following healing affirmations:

> » Jesus' mission was to change relationships, give new purposes, and heal bodies, minds, and spirits. This is our mission, too!
> » Jesus' mission statement was "I have come to give them life – and life in all its abundance." God's abundant life flows in and through us to others, for their health and well-being!
> » Jesus' love – reflecting God's nature and care for humankind – embraced everyone, blamed no one for their illnesses, and broke down barriers of sick and well, and unclean and clean. God's love inspires healing hospitality in and beyond the church!

---

1 For more on the healings of Jesus, see Bruce Epperly *Healing Marks:Healing and Spirituality in Mark's Gospel* (Gonzales, FL: Energion, 2012); *God's Touch: Faith, Wholeness, and the Healing Miracles of Jesus* (Louisville: Westminister/John Knox, 2001); *Healing Worship: Purpose and Practice* (Cleveland: Pilgrim Press, 2006).

Good theology is about affirmations, but there is an implied negation in every positive statement. As I ponder the Acts of the Apostles as a life-giving, healing, spirit-centered gospel for the post-modern world, I believe that in the spirit of Jesus' healing ministry, the following statements ring true for first and twenty-first century followers of the Way of Jesus:

>> Jesus' mission statement – I have come to bring abundant life – says that God is on our side without exception.

>> God's aim at abundant life means God does not cause cancer or heart disease or is the source of traumatic childhoods; God doesn't give us sickness to help us grow, test us, or build character.

>> It also means that God does not punish children because of their parents' sins; punish adults for teenage improprieties; or send floods, earthquakes, or terrorists to punish our country or select cities for immoral behavior.

As Paul states in Romans 8, "in all things God works for good" (Romans 8:28). God doesn't cause illness, death, disease, or pestilence, but is present as the redemptive power in all of these – bringing new energies, awakening possibilities, and helping us recover from life's greatest traumas, whether economic, physical, or spiritual.

EXPECTING GOD'S HEALING TOUCH

Jesus' first followers expected great things from God and great things from themselves. While they lived in a very different world than ourselves – bereft of effective medical care and populated by demonic forces – their experiences still can inspire us. Jesus was a healer and everything he did was intended to change bodies, minds, spirits, relationships, and communities for the best. Following Jesus then and now is more a matter of sharing in his ministry of healing and hospitality than believing abstract doctrines. As we look at our worship and theology, do we expect God to move in the world to bring healing into our lives and the lives of those we love? Do we anticipate the possibility that our prayers will be answered with unexpected recoveries?

We don't need a supernatural overturning of normal causal relationships to take healing seriously. In the quantum universe, creative energy is everywhere. The energy of the first moments of creation, the big bang, still flows through us. Nature itself possesses remarkable and miraculous healing power, revealed in the protective and restorative operation of our immune systems and the gradual healing of wounds. Still, we can pray for something more, and our prayers open the door for God to act in new and surprising ways. Our prayers do not change God's mind or overturn the regularity of nature, and yet they create a healing environment which aids God's own healing purposes.

The gospels and Acts of the Apostles describe a healing partnership which includes personal faith, the belief of friends and family, healing leaders, and God's healing touch. This synergy can transform cells as well as souls, deliver us from unwanted pain and debilitation, and restore our sense of purpose and vocation.

DOES PRAYER MAKE ANY DIFFERENCE?

These days we hear a lot about the power of prayer. Many studies indicate what my physician friends call an "association" between our prayers and the well-being of ourselves and others. Going to church has been found to be a factor in better physical and mental health, recovery from substance abuse, living healthier and longer lives, and responding more positively to illness.[1] This stands to reason: in the interdependent universe, described by contemporary physics, we can imagine our prayers radiating across the universe, surrounding the ones for whom we pray with a positive

1   For more on the positive benefits of religious commitments and the power of prayer, see Harold Koenig, *The Healing Power of Faith* (New York: Simon and Schuster, 2001); Dale Matthews, *The Faith Factor: The Proof of the Healing Power of Prayer* (New York: Penguin, 1999).

field of force and opening the door to a greater influx of God's loving energy. Twice, the gospels record Jesus healing someone at a distance: the servant of a Roman official and the daughter of a Syrophonecian woman.

The first followers of Jesus saturated their lives with prayer. Prayer accompanied every decision and emerged whenever there was a need. In the spirit of the healing of Jairus' daughter, they created healing circles to surround persons in need with God's healing love. They believed great things about God and about our ability to awaken to God's vision and loving power through prayer and faith. While we don't know the exact relationship between the movement described in Acts of the Apostles and the worshiping community led by James, I suspect that James' vision of healing represented practices found among Jesus' earliest followers:

> *Are any among you suffering? They should pray. Are any cheerful? They should sing songs of praise. [14]Are any among you sick? They should call for the elders of the church and have them pray over them, anointing them with oil in the name of the Lord. [15]The prayer of faith will save the sick, and the Lord will raise them up; and anyone who has committed sins will be forgiven. [16]Therefore confess your sins to one another, and pray for one another, so that you may be healed. The prayer of the righteous is powerful and effective.* (James 5:13-16)

These words of James can still serve as a model for congregational healing ministries.

They are grounded in the affirmation of a dynamic synergy intimately joining God and ourselves. While not guaranteeing a cure, the faith of these communities created a field of force that transformed cells as well as souls.

We don't need guarantees or supernaturalism to take healing seriously in the church. We need to embrace and expand our current resources in technological and complementary medicine, the vision that powered those who followed the Way of Jesus:

»   God loves us and seeks our well-being.
»   Our prayers make a difference in an interdependent universe in which mind, body, and spirit are intimately related.
»   Faith, described by medical researchers in terms of the "placebo effect," has physiological effects.
»   Our healing circles are acts of hospitality that transform spirits and, at times, our bodies.
»   God works with and through prayers to bring wholeness to people's lives.
»   God's action, as the healing ministry of Jesus demonstrates, occurs in the context of a call and response in which our faith makes a difference in the nature and impact of God's presence in our lives.

Today's followers of Jesus can creatively embrace high tech and high touch, prayer and Prozac, chanting and chemotherapy, and meditation and medication. Our focus on the interplay of spirituality and healing will be a beacon inviting seekers to join us on the journey.

The earliest Christians took healing seriously. The New Testament narratives as well as accounts from early Christians suggest they also experienced unanswered prayers and more than a few of them died prematurely from illness and persecution. Despite the realities of pain and persecution, they expected great things from God and from the partnership of human faith and divine love. The resurrection power of Jesus lived on, breathing new life into bodies, minds, and spirits.

PRACTICING HEALING PRAYER

What does do the healings from Acts of the Apostles and gospel narratives mean for us here today? How might it change our approach to faith if we believed God seeks healing and wholeness in every situation? Surely, we live in a very different social, economic, scientific, and medical context. We use a different language for diseases than first century Christians: for example, some forms of demon possession are clearly like epilepsy; we would describe the man possessed by a "legion of devils" as suffering from dissociative or multiple personality disorder. Our use of different language in no way undercuts the significance of the first century healing practices. Suffering can be devastating and alienating by whatever name we describe it. Whether we use clinical or ancient language and treat with herbs and touch or pharmaceuticals and laser surgery, serious illness places us in a position of dependency, isolates us from human relationships, and leads us to question the goodness of God and the universe. Unlike first century Christians, we can combine sophisticated technology in diagnosis and treatment. Still, illness drives us to prayer and recovery – whether spiritual, physical, or both – and depends on the presence of caring people, who believe we can be healed and who create healing circles on our behalf. I believe the church is called to be a circle of healing, honoring medicine and embodying God's healing touch. In what ways can you or your congregation become a healing circle and partner in God's quest for Shalom of mind, body, spirit, and relationship?

First, we will take prayer seriously, without predicting the outcome: we will pray for small and large things, anticipating God's care for the whole of our lives. Since many people, like the disciples of old, ask "teach us to pray," our congregations will sponsor courses on prayer, spirituality, and healing that are theologically-sound, spiritually lively, and intensely practical.

Second, we will make healing a priority integrated with worship, Christian education, and mission. In fact, a healing congregation will look for healing opportunities everywhere – in blessing a child during the children's moment; visiting a grieving spouse; creating budgets and making decisions; or sharing in the coffee hour.

Third, we will – through healing prayer – be open to God's healing touch for issues of body, mind, spirit, and relationships, recognizing that nothing is too small or large for God's care.

Finally, we will affirm that when there can't be a physical cure, there can always be healing. Though we seldom think about it, everyone Jesus cured eventually died and the mortality rate remains 100% for humankind regardless of our prayers or medical advances. Churches need to be way stations for pilgrims and their families as they face death, diminishment, and bereavement. As places of hospitality, we do not blame the victim or think of reasons to justify the realities of illness and unanswered prayers. We simply seek to love, bring healing, and surround vulnerable people with compassionate care as they journey toward God's future adventures for them.

The ultimate healing is a relationship with God, in which we experience God's love enfolding us in health and sickness and life and death. With the Dalai Lama, we can affirm that a good life involves being born into loving arms and dying into loving arms. We are resurrection people and we can face death, knowing that love is stronger than death and that nothing in all creation can separate us from the love of God in Christ Jesus, our Lord.

Let me conclude this chapter with the little known, but just as insightful message of the final paragraphs of Reinhold Niebuhr's Serenity Prayer:

> God grant me the serenity
> to accept the things I cannot change;
> courage to change the things I can;
> and wisdom to know the difference.
> Living one day at a time;
> Enjoying one moment at a time;
> Accepting hardships as the pathway to peace;
> Taking, as He did, this sinful world
> as it is, not as I would have it;
> Trusting that He will make all things right
> if I surrender to His Will;
> That I may be reasonably happy in this life
> and supremely happy with Him
> forever in the next. Amen.

TRANSFORMING ACTS

Opening to the Spirit

Intercessory and petitionary prayers are at the heart of Christian spirituality. Jesus invites as to ask, seek, and knock. James counsels that every season of life – positive or negative – can be an occasion for prayer. We pray for what we want or for our concerns for others and often discover the deeper truths of what we and others need in the larger scheme of God's relationship with the world. Anglican Bishop Temple asserted that "when I pray, coincidences happen, and when I don't, they don't." New Testament scholar and spiritual leader Walter Wink noted that the future belongs to the intercessors. While answers to our prayers are not guaranteed, our prayers deepen our sense of God's presence, open us to our deepest desires often hidden in our prayers, connect us with others, and create the possibility of greater influxes of divine power and presence.

In light of the healing ministry of the first Christians, make a commitment to pray for events large and small. Begin the day with gratitude and requests for wisdom. Ask for divine insight when you make decisions. Pray for people in physical, spiritual, emotional, or relational need. Join the Spirit in prayers of intercession for your deepest needs and the needs of those around you.

A bench at Kirkridge Retreat Center in Bangor, Pennsylvania proclaims, "Picket and Pray." Our prayers invite us to social involvement and justice-seeking. The quest for justice is part of God's aim at healing, and in insuring social and economic justice and equality, we actually prevent illnesses of body, mind, and spirit.

Transforming Affirmations

Spiritual affirmations awaken us to the God's Spirit moving through our lives and the world.

In the days ahead, consider the following healing affirmations:

God's healing light flows in and through me, bringing wholeness to my life and those whom I touch.
I open myself to God's healing energy in every encounter.
I share God's healing touch with everyone I meet.

Manifesting Mission

Mission takes many forms, but ultimately involves the interplay of spirituality and action. Our inner journey issues in an outer journey that touches peoples' lives and invites them to share in God's grace at the personal or community levels.

If your congregation has a healing worship service, consider becoming part of the healing team. Ideally, every congregation should spend time in prayer and study as it prepares to manifest God's healing love. Take time to read books on healing, wholeness, and prayer.

If your congregation does not have a healing worship service, consider ways that you might be a catalyst for conversation. What's standing in the way of a healing ministry – theologically, liturgically, or practically? How might such a service reflect your congregation's worship style and theology? The service does not need to be numerically significant to be important in the life of the church. Its presence will attract persons who recognize their vulnerability and needs. We cannot predict what happens when we pray or practice laying on of hands, but we can pray together as an act of love and a way to share God's healing presence with people in need. More often than not, people experience gradual healings or greater peace that enables them to deal with life's challenges. On occasion, someone will experience a quantum leap of divine energy that brings about an alleviation of suffering or cures an ailment. Regardless of the outcome, healing worship services are acts of love that bring wholeness and welcome to those for whom we pray.

SIX

Spirit-Centered Leadership

Now during those days, when the disciples were increasing in number, the Hellenists complained against the Hebrews because their widows were being neglected in the daily distribution of food. ²And the twelve called together the whole community of the disciples and said, "It is not right that we should neglect the word of God in order to wait at tables. ³Therefore, friends, select from among yourselves seven men of good standing, full of the Spirit and of wisdom, whom we may appoint to this task, ⁴while we, for our part, will devote ourselves to prayer and to serving the word." ⁵What they said pleased the whole community, and they chose Stephen, a man full of faith and the Holy Spirit, together with Philip, Prochorus, Nicanor, Timon, Parmenas, and Nicolaus, a proselyte of Antioch. ⁶They had these men stand before the apostles, who prayed and laid their hands on them. ⁷The word of God continued to spread; the number of the disciples increased greatly in Jerusalem, and a great many of the priests became obedient to the faith. (Acts 6:1-7)

Trouble in Paradise

"And they shared their meals with glad and generous hearts" characterized the Christian community in those glorious days following Pentecost. The community was still small in numbers and was characterized by face-to-face encounters. In that honeymoon of the spirit, the early Christians sold their possessions, and insured that everyone had what they needed in terms of food and housing. Spiritual experiences led them to see their self-interest as embracing the well-being of the whole community, regardless of ethnicity, age, gender, and economics. If the Spirit inspires everyone, then everyone deserves ethical consideration and adequate food, lodging, and support.

But, like most real life honeymoons, this honeymoon of the spirit didn't last forever. Lovers discover that being in love isn't always about moonlight walks, dinner and a movie, and wandering aimlessly about town hugging and holding hands, although that can still persist in a long-term relationship. Eventually, if love leads to a committed relationship, a couple may discover that healthy relationships involve finances, mortgages, putting out the garbage and recycle bin, changing diapers and carpooling to school, as well as moments of romance. They have to move on to the challenging but joyful work of making a marriage or partnership work. Our hope, of course, is that we do these ordinary things in extraordinary ways, and grow in love for one another in the everyday tasks of housekeeping and working, and caring for children and the wider community. In fact, a good life and growing relationship involves good work, joyful moments, and domestic chores that bring health, safety, and well-being to those we love, even if we have to make personal sacrifices.

Well, spiritual honeymoons don't last forever either – or at least, they change shape over time. The ecstatic Pentecostal vision, the lively worship, the shared meals, and generosity must be lived out in ordinary life day after day and month after month, and – just like a committed relationship – it is inevitable that conflicts emerge. How we respond to these conflicts can deepen or destroy a community or relationship.

Recently, I heard an interview with a scientist regarding global climate change, often described popularly, though inaccurately, as global warming. She noted that as we look at small changes in temperature that may lead to potentially large changes in weather systems, we cannot evade or deny, but must transform. Or, as the apostle Paul affirmed in Romans 12:2, "Be not conformed to this world but be transformed by the renewing of your mind." Still enlivened by the fire and winds of Pentecost, the early Christians discovered much to their surprise that there was trouble in paradise!

As the community grew, their face-to- face informal patterns of leadership no longer worked. As the scripture says, "a complaint arose. Greek speaking disciples accused the majority Aramaic disciples because their widows were being overlooked in the daily food service." I am sure that this was not intentional. I suspect that the spiritual leadership assumed that everyone was being fed, when in fact some had to beg and borrow simply to get by from day to day. Worse yet, those who struggled to make ends meet came from the minority membership of the community, Greek-speaking Jews. Was the church inadvertently repeating old patterns of ethnic injustice and exclusion?

REIMAGINING LEADERSHIP

No doubt, the spiritual leaders were appalled and apologized for their omission, but apologies aren't enough – good intentions aren't enough – when people are suffering, especially as a result of our neglect or inaction. Faced with complaints drawn up on racial lines, they could have denied that there was a problem or passed the problem down the road. They might even, as some have done throughout history, blamed the victims for their misfortune and poverty or accused the complainants of being insubordinate and uppity purveyors of class warfare! Instead, they did something essential to spirit-centered leadership: they allowed themselves to be transformed and in so doing transformed the community. They recognized the importance of their vocation as spiritual leaders and their limitations in time, attention, and energy.

The spiritual leaders acknowledged that they couldn't do everything. They confessed that the task of sharing God's word left no time for taking care of domestic issues. They needed partners in ministry: so they prayerfully chose a group of people to insure that everyone had a share in the community's resources. They let go of control, and let go of power, so that human needs could be met. In ways that are still countercultural, they relinquished the power of the purse for a greater good, the well-being of the whole people of God. They recognized that within the body of Christ, everyone has a role – their spiritual leadership of the community did not lead to micromanaging or power plays, or a sense of spiritual superiority, but a vision of shared responsibility. Perhaps, their selfless leadership inspired the Apostle Paul's vision of the multi-gifted body of Christ in which the well-being of one shapes the health of the whole body and the whole body, operating effectively, provides nurture and support for each constituent part.

THEOLOGY AND SPIRIT-CENTERED LEADERSHIP

The leaders of the Jerusalem community walked the talk. They lived out their theological visions in the gritty business of leadership and administration. Have you ever noticed a profound disconnect between some peoples' beliefs about God and their behavior as leaders and administrators? They may invoke a loving God, but their leadership is unilateral and inflexible. They may affirm God's generous care, but live solely by the bottom line, forgetting that God has promised to supply our deepest needs. Too often, it seems that Christians become "practical atheists" the minute the budget or personnel issues are discussed!

The spiritual leaders believed that the Spirit of God had touched everyone in the community. They believed that God was active in their lives, the source of healing energy and abundant living. Trusting the God of abundance and generosity, they were confident that they could share power with others, respect others' leadership, and commit themselves to their calling recognizing the importance of others' vocations in the community.

While not exhaustive, the first century Christian movement gives us some images of spirit-centered leadership. *First*, spirit-centered leaders listen, especially to unfamiliar and sometimes critical voices. They see diverse viewpoints as an opportunity for creative change and embrace otherness rather than deny, silence, or avoid it. They are willing to confess their failures and make changes in light of the pain, injustice, and neglect others feel.

Second, they recognize that God is in the details. Nothing is exempt from God's concern. We can practice the presence of God as easily in the kitchen or buying groceries, to invoke the wisdom of Brother Lawrence, as at times of prayer, worship, and communion. Brick and mortar, budgets and toilet paper, are also spiritual issues. A wonderful program can be sabotaged by poor administration. Let me share a down to earth story from my own experience as a spiritual leader. In my position as an administrator at Lancaster Seminary, I was in charge of lectures and conferences that often brought large groups to campus. Knowing the importance of small details, I made it a practice early in the morning of each program to check the restrooms to insure we had enough toilet paper. I asked my female staff members to check the women's restrooms throughout the day. Such attention to detail sounds very intellectual, doesn't it? It's real professorial work, right? But, running out of toilet paper can undermine the quality of an event. No detail is too small – or too large – when we are seeking excellence in serving God. In fact, if God is omnipresent, moving through all things great and small, then our care for small details is one way to do something beautiful for God.

Third, the spiritual leaders acted prayerfully and collaboratively. Sometimes we need a few minutes to gain perspective and wisdom about a decision. The apostles took the issue of food supply to God and the whole community, looking for guidance and insight to respond to the problem and find new partners in ministry. They trusted God's inspiration in their lives but they also realized that they needed to check their insights with the whole community of disciples, especially those whose ethnic group had been neglected.

Fourth, they recognized that every task in the body of Christ is spiritual. Sometimes the most ordinary tasks are the most important to the survival of a community. Sometimes the unsung heroes are not noticed, but their devotion insures our success. We don't always see the housekeeping and maintenance staff or volunteers at church functions, but without their expertise, we would be overwhelmed by details and unable to perform our tasks with excellence. We all have vocations and having different vocations is not a matter of superior or inferior but passion and talent.

Fifth, spirit-led leadership is appreciative and affirmative: it notices who's doing what, expresses gratitude, and notes success. It takes nothing for granted, but recognizes that we all matter – we all have gifts – and we all deserve thanks.

Sixth, spirit-centered leadership is creative and innovative. It looks for solutions rather than problems. It doesn't make excuses: it takes responsibility and makes changes. The apostles could have made excuses or dismissed their critics. Instead, they stated clearly their mission and then found a way to bring others on board to fulfill the mission of responding to physical as well as spiritual needs of the Gentile families. Disaster and division were averted in Jerusalem because of the practical spirituality of those first leaders.

Finally, spirit-centered leadership is visionary. It has a fluid, concrete, and imaginative vision that guides everything we do. For Jesus it was: "I came that they might have life, and life in all its abundance." This vision statement guided his many, dynamic, concrete interactions – healing, teaching, welcoming, and mentoring. What is your personal and congregational vision statement? Does it guide your vocation on the job and at home?

Conflict and challenge are essential to life, and change is inevitable; but when we open to the spirit, as Acts proclaims, "God's word will continue to grow" – in the hearts of children, in adults who experience new life, in welcoming the unemployed and vulnerable, and in sharing good news day by day that lasts a lifetime and beyond. Thanks be to God for the Spirit that inspires, energizes, and guides.

TRANSFORMING ACTS

Opening to the Spirit

The spiritual leaders of the Christian community responded to conflict with a spiritual practice that I identify with the work of psychiatrist-spiritual guide Gerald May: *pause, notice, open, yield* and *stretch,* and then *respond.* As I stated earlier in this text, this is a good way to respond to any life situation. Rather than defensiveness, anger, or denial, take time to experience what's going on without judgment; let the experience change you and call you to greater stature, and then respond prayerfully.

Conflict is universal and, eventually, whether you deny it, sublimate it, avoid it, or defeat it, eventually you will have to face it. Conflict is not always a bad thing: in fact, as church leader, Chris Hobgood asserts, "resistance" is a sign that you are trying to be innovative or altar less than optimal practices or behaviors.[1] We can prayerfully prepare for conflict in everyday decision-making and conversational situations by taking time to do the following spiritual exercise:

> » *Pause* to listen to what's being said or done. "Don't say something, listen," letting go of judgment or the desire for a quick response.
> » *Notice* what's going on and your initial emotional or intellectual response.
> » *Open* to the whole range of experiences, your experience and others.
> » *Yield* and stretch, accept what's going on without judgment and let it invite you to growth.
> » *Respond* in ways that assure another that he or she has been heard and that brings healing, joy, unity, or reconciliation to the situation.

This doesn't mean agreement or acceptance of certain behaviors, but it does mean experiencing what's really going on and discovering a creative and prayerful response.

---

1 W. Chris Hobgood, *Welcoming Resistance* (Herndon, VA: Alban Institute, 2002).

Transforming Affirmations

Many of us are afraid of conflict as a result of our family of origins. As a child, my brother's outbursts filled me with fear and dread. Though he never physically harmed me, his tantrums felt threatening to me. As an adult, I still felt those same feelings of fear and danger anytime someone raised their voice. One of the ways, besides spending time in therapy, spiritual direction, and self-examination, I have learned to creatively respond to those visceral feelings is through the use of affirmations, such as:

Nothing can separate me from the love God, not even this conflict situation.
God is giving me good ideas to respond creatively to this situation.
I have all the resources I need to find a solution that brings change, healing, and reconciliation.

Manifesting Mission

Mission takes many forms. It is the outer expression of our personal and community faith and values. The Acts community had a strong sense of God's presence in every life, reflected in their affirmation that salvation and inspiration were available to all people, beginning with everyone in the Jewish community and then the whole world. Everyone is God's beloved child, worthy of grace and love. They saw differently and then acted differently. I suspect despite their feelings of discomfort and sorrow at the pain of the Greek-speaking followers of Jesus, the spiritual leaders were able to let go of defensiveness and listen creatively to complaints because they saw the Hellenistic Christians as God's beloved children and vehicles of divine wisdom. In honoring who they were, they were led to expansive actions of supportive and transformational leadership.

Commit yourself to seeing the holiness of everyone you meet. Put on the vision of Christ, seeing God – as Mother Teresa says – in all of God's distressing and, I would add, various disguises. Move from seeing to acting, treating everyone you meet at church, home, work, the market, or on the highway as God's beloved child.

SEVEN

FAITH WITHOUT
FENCES

Then an angel of the Lord said to Philip, "Get up and go towards the south to the road that goes down from Jerusalem to Gaza." (This is a wilderness road.) ²⁷So he got up and went. Now there was an Ethiopian eunuch, a court official of the Candace, queen of the Ethiopians, in charge of her entire treasury. He had come to Jerusalem to worship ²⁸and was returning home; seated in his chariot, he was reading the prophet Isaiah. ²⁹Then the Spirit said to Philip, "Go over to this chariot and join it." ³⁰So Philip ran up to it and heard him reading the prophet Isaiah. He asked, "Do you understand what you are reading?" ³¹He replied, "How can I, unless someone guides me?" And he invited Philip to get in and sit beside him.... ³⁵Then Philip began to speak, and starting with this scripture, he proclaimed to him the good news about Jesus. ³⁶As they were going along the road, they came to some water; and the eunuch said, "Look, here is water! What is to prevent me from being baptized?" ³⁸He commanded the chariot to stop, and both of them, Philip and the eunuch, went down into the water, and Philip* baptized him. ³⁹When they came up out of the water, the Spirit of the Lord snatched Philip away; the eunuch saw him no more, and went on his way rejoicing. ⁴⁰But Philip found himself at Azotus, and as he was passing through the region, he proclaimed the good news to all the towns until he came to Caesarea. (Acts 8:26-31, 35-40)

NO BOUNDARIES

Have any of you read the cartoon series "Kudzu" by Doug Marlette that ran in syndication in many newspapers from 1981-2007? If you have, you might remember the "Rev. Will B. Dunn."

Believe it or not, he was patterned after one of my ministerial heroes, Will Campbell, a Southern Baptist pastor, whose demeanor and iconoclasm were a lot like John the Baptist's.

In the early 1950's, Campbell served as chaplain at "Ole Miss," the University of Mississippi. He thought he'd spend a lifetime in that prestigious position, but left after two years – due to receiving numerous death threats for his support of desegregating the university. In the 50's and 60's he marched with Martin Luther King, protested the Vietnam war, was the only white person present at the founding of the Southern Leadership Conference, and was one of four persons to walk to the school door with the black students who integrated the Little Rock public schools.

He was darling of the political and religious left until he reached out to members of the Ku Klux Klan, most of whom were lower middle class whites, serving them communion, marrying and burying, and even – according to legend – celebrating communion with a bottle of bourbon with Bob Jones, Grand Dragon of the North Carolina Ku Klux Klan, the night before he was sent off to prison for contempt of Congress. Campbell noted somewhat ironically: "It's been a long time since I got a hate letter from the right. Now they come from the left."

Campbell was uncompromising in his theology. God loves the immortal soul of the oppressed and also loves the immortal soul of the oppressor. God's love embraces those who simply hate because they don't know anything different, the unknowing victims of the same forces that insure that both they and the African Americans who they fear and hate are unable to secure a living wage. God loves those for whom we advocate and those whom we oppose for their racism and injustice.

No doubt Philip felt the same way when he encountered the Ethiopian eunuch. Despite the fact the Ethiopian followed the God of the Jewish people, he was not really Jewish and could never fully be. In fact, he was a double outcast and second class citizen: he belonged to another ethnic group and because of his sexuality, having been castrated, he was condemned by scripture and placed beyond the boundaries of the community of faith and God's realm of salvation. According to the injunctions of Deuteronomy 23:1, "No one whose testicles are crushed or whose penis is cut off shall be admitted to the assembly of the LORD."

Sometimes we have to practice what we preach and we have to walk the talk. This was Philip's challenge: he had been there at Pentecost where he experienced God's universal love, embracing young and old, woman and man, slave and free, Jew and Gentile. But now he was face to face with an outcast – how he knew of the Ethiopian's status remains a mystery! – he would have to live the faith he affirmed.

God's Spirit had already led Philip beyond Judea. Philip expanded the circle of God's love when he crossed the border into Samaria and ministered to a racial group that Jewish people saw as inferior in ethnicity and religion. Do you remember Jesus' Parable of the Good Samaritan and how scandalous it must have been for Jesus' audience? But, then the Spirit inspired Philip to make the circle of grace even wider as the Spirit's gentle but persistent power guided him to take a wilderness road to Gaza, which – if you read the news – is currently a place of violence and unrest among Jews and Palestinians. There he encounters a wealthy African, reading scripture, trying to make sense of a passage from the prophet Isaiah. The two mean enter into conversation, motivated by the Ethiopian's questions.

As they continue along, the Ethiopian spies an oasis and asks Philip, "what would hinder me from being baptized?" Once again, in Acts of the Apostles, we discover that God's grace is unhindered, the outsider is welcomed and the gospel is proclaimed. The man is not coerced or intimidated or threatened with hell. In fact, Philip lets the Ethiopian lead the way, responding to him and ministering to his expressed needs, rather than imposing his will upon him.

GOOD NEWS GIVEN GRACEFULLY

Good news sharing – evangelism – is not about fear or control, but responding to the needs of those around us, letting them guide us in the way we will share the gospel. In behavior similar to the Jerusalem leader's response to the challenges of insuring that everyone be treated fairly in the growing community, Philip listened to the Ethiopian, realizing that it was more important for this new believer to assert himself and to claim his power as a follower of Jesus than for Philip to determine the man's initiation into the Christian community. Philip may have remembered Jesus' own approach to persons in need of physical and spiritual counsel: "What do you want me to do for you?" Jesus asks Bartimaeus (Mark 10:46-52). "Do you want to be made well?" Jesus inquires of a man who had been paralyzed for nearly forty years (John 5:6).

The story of Philip and the Ethiopian eunuch reminds me of the origins of the American denomination, the Christian Church (Disciples of Christ). From the very beginning, Disciples of Christ have practiced open communion and have been a model for the ecumenical movement's communion hospitality. In the early nineteenth century, Thomas Campbell, a newcomer to the United States from Ireland, was appalled by sectarianism among religious groups in the new nation. Even Presbyterians from different sects would not take communion with one another. Inspired by his vision of the New Testament church, Campbell welcomed everyone to the Communion Table. "Don't fence the table," he proclaimed. "Anyone who seeks to follow Jesus as the Christ is welcome, regardless of denominational background." As early Disciples of Christ proclaimed: "We have no creed but Christ." Our unity in Christ and our allegiance to Christ compels us to expand the circle of his love to include everyone.

Like every emerging movement, the early Christian movement struggled with how wide the circle of welcome should be, but eventually sided with Philip, Peter, and Paul in proclaiming the unhindered gospel. Everyone is welcome, everyone belongs, and everyone can share the good news.

Acts of the Apostles challenges us to proclaim a faith without fences. As we look at the world around us, we can affirm that diversity of flora and fauna, ethnicity, culture, and even religion is blessed by God. Any student of Christian history will soon discover that Christianity is not a homogeneous movement in which one faith and practice fits all, but a glorious canvass of diverse approaches to God, worship, structure, and doctrine. While we as Christians have every right to affirm our particular tradition's gifts and identity, our goal should be to include rather than exclude. With the first Christians, we need to recognize that God is still speaking and that we grow in wisdom and stature in faithful dialogue with the varieties of Christian as well as the global spiritual experience. As a Christian you can be both/and: a progressive and a Pentecostal, evangelical spirited and socially active, formal in worship style and emotional in fervor, a justice seeker and a contemplative, committed to scripture and welcoming of outsiders, including gay and lesbian persons.

Although I seek to be hospitable to the varieties of Christian and interfaith experiences, in the course of this book, I've made numerous theological statements that reflect my beliefs that:

» God is still speaking in our lives
» We can experience moments of mysticism and life-changing encounters with God
» God calls us to grow together, embracing truth wherever it is found
» Each person has a vocation in the body of Christ
» God speaks to each one of us, calling us to be God's partners in healing the world
» Our actions truly matter, especially to God and the future of our planet

»   We can shape each other's lives by our actions, promoting healing and wholeness through touch, prayer, and welcome

»   God loves diversity of all kinds, ethnic, cultural, religious, sexual, biological, and environment

»   We can open the door to experiencing God through spiritual practices which inspire mission in the larger community

These beliefs are a matter of life and death for me. They express my experience of God and God's ever-widening compass of divine grace, salvation, and love. But, I recognize that other Christians take contrasting approaches to life's most important questions. They understand God's power as sovereign and all-determining in contrast to my vision of God's power as relational and inspirational. They believe God is the source of good and evil alike while I affirm that God seeks abundant life for everyone. Our beliefs are radically different; still I can affirm them as Christian brothers and sisters and seek to gain wisdom from their insights.

Earlier in this text, I asserted that God can be poetically described as "a circle whose center is everywhere and whose circumference is nowhere." This affirmation enables me to rejoice in my place at the center of God's love and see everyone else at the center as well.

I have spent a good deal of time at Benedictine Monasteries and in virtually every monastery I have seen the counsel "treat everyone as Christ." This is really the heart of Christian hospitality – grounded in Matthew 25, "as you have done to the least of these, you have done to me." This was the hospitality that led Philip to preach good news in Samaria and then to accept the eunuch's invitation.

The passage from Acts concludes with a curious comment: "When they came up out of the water, the Spirit of the Lord snatched Philip away; the eunuch saw him no more, and went on his way rejoicing. But Philip found himself at Azotus, and as he was passing through the region, he proclaimed the good news to all the towns until he came to Caesarea" (Acts 8:40). Following the Way of Jesus leads to strange adventures in unexpected places; for those who open themselves to the ever-widening circle of God's love, every place is home and every person a fellow pilgrim on our journey with God.

TRANSFORMING ACTS

Opening to the Spirit

The psychologist and psychiatrist Carl Jung described "synchronicity" or meaningful coincidence as one of the ways persons grow spiritually. Strewn across our lives are unexpected encounters that can change everything for those whose senses and hearts are open.

An ancient philosopher noted that "if you don't expect the unexpected, you will never find it." The same applies to God-encounters. Keep your senses open and look for angels unaware and opportunities to reach out throughout the day, and your life will be an adventure in companionship with God and God's children.

Transforming Affirmations

Affirmations enable us to respond creatively to the holy otherness of strangers and challenging persons. They help us move spiritually from suspicion, fear, and antagonism to respect and hospitality. They may even transform others' attitudes toward us.

I see the holiness of everyone I meet.
Strangers are opportunities to make new friends and learn new things.
I am open to seeing Christ in all of Christ's strange and sometimes challenging disguises.

Manifesting Mission

In Marilynne Robinson's prize-winning novel, *Gilead*, the main character Pastor John Ames, a small town Congregationalist minister, states that his primary vocation as a minister is to "bless." To bless is to proclaim God's love and care on another person, whether friend or stranger. Blessing, however, is not just the work of an ordained minister; it is the vocation of the whole people of God.

Mission can take many forms, one of which is our treatment and attitudes toward others. We can live a life of blessing or cursing. Living a life of blessing means that you silently send God's care to everyone you meet, regardless of the circumstances. At first, you find this spiritual discipline challenging. After all, it is very easy to curse drivers who cut in front of you on the freeway, store clerks who make you wait in line while they talk on their cell phones, politicians who advocate policies that are reprehensible to you, leaders of nations that threaten our security, or family members who fail to respect our needs. Blessing looks beyond the face and the act to see the holiness of others and bring it out. Acts of blessing may not change others' behavior or the external circumstances of our lives, but they will change our attitude and relationships and quite possibly everything.

Make a commitment to quietly bless everyone you meet. If it is appropriate for you to do so, say "bless you" or "God bless you" or a word of kindness to others. Let this be an experiment in spiritual transformation. See what happens when you live a life of blessing. You may discover that blessing leads to concrete actions that improve peoples' lives and economic welfare. In blessing the earth, you may be inspired to act in response to global climate change and painful condition of animals in factory farms. In blessing other persons, you may be inspired to embrace a spirituality and politics of compassion that seeks to add beauty to the world by improving the conditions of all God's children.

EIGHT

MYSTICISM AND MISSION

Meanwhile Saul, still breathing threats and murder against the disciples of the Lord, went to the high priest [2]and asked him for letters to the synagogues at Damascus, so that if he found any who belonged to the Way, men or women, he might bring them bound to Jerusalem. [3]Now as he was going along and approaching Damascus, suddenly a light from heaven flashed around him. [4]He fell to the ground and heard a voice saying to him, "Saul, Saul, why do you persecute me?" [5]He asked, "Who are you, Lord?" The reply came, "I am Jesus, whom you are persecuting. [6]But get up and enter the city, and you will be told what you are to do." [7]The men who were travelling with him stood speechless because they heard the voice but saw no one. [8]Saul got up from the ground, and though his eyes were open, he could see nothing; so they led him by the hand and brought him into Damascus. [9]For three days he was without sight, and neither ate nor drank.

[10] Now there was a disciple in Damascus named Ananias. The Lord said to him in a vision, "Ananias." He answered, "Here I am, Lord." [11]The Lord said to him, "Get up and go to the street called Straight, and at the house of Judas look for a man of Tarsus named Saul. At this moment he is praying, [12]and he has seen in a vision a man named Ananias come in and lay his hands on him so that he might regain his sight." [13]But Ananias answered, "Lord, I have heard from many about this man, how much evil he has done to your saints in Jerusalem; [14]and here he has authority from the chief priests to bind all who invoke your name." [15]But the Lord said to him, "Go, for he is an instrument whom I have chosen to bring my name before Gentiles and kings and before the people of Israel; [16]I myself will show him how much he must suffer for the sake of my name." [17]So Ananias went and entered the house. He laid his hands on Saul and said, "Brother Saul,

the Lord Jesus, who appeared to you on your way here, has sent me
so that you may regain your sight and be filled with the Holy Spirit."
[18]And immediately something like scales fell from his eyes, and his sight
was restored. Then he got up and was baptized, [19]and after taking some
food, he regained his strength.

For several days he was with the disciples in Damascus, [20]and
immediately he began to proclaim Jesus in the synagogues, saying, "He
is the Son of God." [21]All who heard him were amazed and said, "Is
not this the man who made havoc in Jerusalem among those who in-
voked this name? And has he not come here for the purpose of bringing
them bound before the chief priests?" [22]Saul became increasingly more
powerful and confounded the Jews who lived in Damascus by proving
that Jesus was the Messiah. (Acts 9:1-22)

AN INVITATION TO THE WAY

The words of the hymn "Amazing Grace" are an apt description
of Paul's experience of creative transformation and new orientation.
"I once was lost, but now I'm found, was blind, but now I see."
Though Paul often dismisses his ardor as a Pharisee as "filthy rags,"
he was a truly good person, a follower of the God of Israel and obedient to the laws of his people; but his goodness was not enough
to save him. He needed an encounter with the Light of Creation
and Healing, Jesus the Christ.

We probably know more about the Apostle Paul than anyone
in scripture, with perhaps the exception of Jesus, Moses, and David. Paul describes his spiritual journey and current state of affairs
throughout his letters and in the two speeches in Acts (22:6-21;
26:12-18) which describe his mystical encounter with Jesus on the
road to Damascus.

Paul's Damascus road experience is important for a variety
of reasons. First, it is one of the most detailed autobiographical
descriptions of an encounter with God in scripture. Paul's tells his
story of finding a new vision of God and new way of life. Second,
it has served as a model for certain types of Christian experienc-

es throughout history: the datable, emotional, transformational "come to Jesus" moments in which we must die to an old life and begin a new one. Some people believe that the only authentic Christians are those who can affirm an "hour I first believed." While born again experiences transform our lives, they are surely not the only model for Christian tradition. To absolutize one particular experience is to go against God's own personal relationship with each of us and to deny God's affirmation of diversity in spiritual experiences and expressions of faith.

Such dramatic experiences – whether evangelical or mystical in nature – are not normative for all Christians. Some of us are born Christian. As cradle Christians, we are dedicated or baptized as infants, and then grow in grace not by drama but through a gentle, day to day walk with God. Nevertheless, most of us eventually face moments in which we have to say "no" to one way of life – or certain behaviors or lifestyles – to say "yes" to another.

Providence is both gentle and dramatic. We can experience God, while we are playing with our children and looking across the table at a beloved spouse or friend; we may also discover God in the storms of life, helpless yet saved by a power beyond ourselves.

Third, Paul's Damascus road experience invites us to connect our spiritual experiences, whether at worship, at camp, or on the road, with discovering our vocation and mission in life. Paul is clear that his mystical experience was not an end in itself, but an invitation to a new self-understanding and vocation as God's messenger to the Gentile world.

My Goodness!

Now, despite his own confessions as the worst of sinners, Paul was a very religious person. He was Pharisee, a teacher, a rabbi. He was careful to observe all the rules of his faith without exception. No doubt, he was being groomed for what today we would describe as a large pulpit in a high steeple church, if not a bishop or denominational leader. His hatred, even violence toward the

Jesus movement was not motivated by evil or a desire for power, but by his fears. Somehow this new movement emerging in the Jewish community might corrupt or displace the "old time religion" founded on Mount Sinai or the religion of law and ethnicity, of behaviors that defined Jews as separate and unique in the pluralistic world of the Roman Empire. Paul viewed with horror the growing universalism among Jesus' Jewish followers as a threat to the necessary boundaries of Jew and Gentile, woman and man, unclean and clean. Such violations might lead to even greater acts of divine punishment than the Jews had already received at the hands of Rome.

But, if we trust of some of Paul's own autobiographical comments, his scrupulous and unbending legalism did not bring him spiritual contentment. In fact, deep down he was torn and may have rebelled, in the privacy of his own heart or the cloak of darkness, against the religious laws that were so dear to his heart and that defined his identity. Paul confesses that:

Now if I do what I do not want, I agree that the law is good. [17]But in fact it is no longer I that do it, but sin that dwells within me. [18]For I know that nothing good dwells within me, that is, in my flesh. I can will what is right, but I cannot do it. [19]For I do not do the good I want, but the evil I do not want is what I do. [20]Now if I do what I do not want, it is no longer I that do it, but sin that dwells within me....Wretched man that I am! .Who will rescue me from this body of death? [25]Thanks be to God through Jesus Christ our Lord! (Romans 7:16-20, 24-25a)

Paul's inner turmoil may have fueled his hatred for the Jesus movement and its relaxed boundaries, words of grace, and willingness to accept all comers, clean and unclean, tax collector and woman of ill repute, oppressor and revolutionary. Like the older brother in the parable of the prodigal son, his alienation from this spiritual movement may have risen from his envy of their joy and freedom in contrast to the burdens the law placed upon his heart and mind. As the hymn goes, "Twas grace that taught my heart to

fear": grace can be too much, forgiveness too fearsome, acceptance
and hospitality too frightening to those for whom rigidity defines
their life. After all, Paul and other adherents of orthodoxy have
asked: What do we have, if we bend the rules and open the club of
salvation to strangers? What is the meaning of our faith if sinners
can be saved, too? Does our relationship to Jesus and quest for
virtue mean anything if God widens the circle of grace to include
Hindus, Buddhists, Sikhs, Jews, Muslims, and other seekers? If
there's no reward to be secured or punishment to be avoided by
confessing Jesus as savior or following God's law, what's the incen-
tive for becoming a Christian?

BLINDED BY THE LIGHT

So Paul travels to Damascus, a religious district attorney ready-
to indict and arrest Jewish followers of the way of Jesus. He believes
that his only salvation and the salvation of this people is the oblit-
eration of this new and heretic faith, with its vision of freedom and
hospitality. In the course of our lives, grace comes when we seek it;
but it also comes unexpectedly when we're running in the opposite
direction. Paul encounters a great light and a voice; they envelope
him, leave him confused and blind. Once self-reliant, he is now
helpless, depending on others to find his way.

At virtually the same time, Ananias, a leader among the followers of Jesus, has a vision and receives guidance to seek out Saul
(Paul's birth name). Ananias is, rightfully, apprehensive and questions the divine guidance he receives. In response, the voice in the
vision reveals Paul's ultimate identity – not as a persecutor, but as
a proclaimer. Ironically, the most orthodox of Jews, one who dis-
trusted foreigners, and the blood-thirsty antagonist who detested
the universalism of Jesus' followers, will become the primary messenger of good news to the Gentiles and the primary proponent
of a grace that not only bends but transforms the rules of faith. In
fact, some historians have described Paul as the second founder of
Christianity, the one whose voice structured and defined the mes-

sage of Jesus for the Gentile world. The one whose mission to the Gentiles and advocacy for a global faith is responsible for many of us having heard the good news of God's grace.

Later, in reflecting on this experience, Paul senses that God had been with him all along. Providentially, God had moved in Paul's upbringing, Roman citizenship, theological education, and even his alienation from Jesus to bring him to this critical moment of transformation and a future of spiritual leadership. All through his life God had been present, luring him to a place of crisis and healing, and a vocation that would change the world. I am sure that Paul had the freedom to say "yes" or "no" throughout his life. But, even when he turned from the new creation in Christ and Christ's followers, God was moving through his "no" toward a world-shaping "yes!"

At this point, I must add that neither Paul the apostle nor God the Creative One turned their backs on the Jewish people. God's universal love, so transformative Paul's life, is alive and well among our Jewish friends, inspiring them to faithful partnership and us to faithful affirmation in God's quest to heal the world. Grace is all-embracing, and there is no room for anti-Judaism – or demeaning of any other religious tradition – within the all-embracing love of God.

SPIRITUAL AND RELIGIOUS!

Today, according to surveys, 30% of adults in the USA and 40% of Canadians describe themselves as "spiritual but not religious." They contrast the freedom of a spiritual experience with the rigidity and legalism of what they believe characterizes organized religion. While many of their definitions of spirituality appear vague and superficial, their experiences represent a deep hunger to experience holiness and wholeness in a technological world as well as a challenge to Christian churches to become centers of spiritual growth.

Paul's Damascus experience enables him to become both "spiritual and religious." He experiences the freedom of new creation, honors the traditions of Judaism, and grounds that freedom in a relationship with Jesus and the way of his followers. He helps create a structure, but the structure is freeing and innovative, not legalistic and backward-looking.

On the road to Damascus, Paul experiences a conversion, a radical spiritual transformation, not from unfaith to faith, but from a rigid, rule-oriented faith to a lively, creative, free-spirited faith. He receives a new name – Saul becomes Paul – and a new job description, apostle of Jesus Christ. He receives a commission – a vocation or calling – to share good news with the Gentile world, to make the message of Christ accessible to everyone – male or female, Jew or Greek, old or young, slave or free, sinner or righteous. All need grace, and all need to hear good news.

Today, Paul's experience calls us to join our own spirituality with mission. We don't have to wait for a blinding light: we might simply ask "God, what do you want me to do to be more faithful? Jesus, what is my vocation, my calling, in this time? What rigid behaviors and rules do I need to let go to be faithful to you?"

Now, we all have many callings – parent, child, adult child with aging parents, professional, student, friend, but through all of these diverse callings, God invites us to see the light within ourselves and the world. God invites us to experience God's light in the faces of others and to bring forth God's light in our parenting, workplaces, as we dance and play, and as we serve others in our community and in the larger world. Light must shine to be light, and from that light on Damascus Road, Saul now Paul became a light giver everywhere. Every moment can be a mission and opportunity to be part of God's synchronicity of grace.

On the road, every day, let us see the light, the wonder, beauty, and spirit of life that makes each day an adventure; and let us bear that light so others might find joy, meaning, friendship, the love of Jesus, and the resources to live well, grow up strong, and take care of our families and join in God's movement of grace.

TRANSFORMING ACTS

Opening to the Spirit

I appreciate the point-counterpoint of two wise sayings from Frederick Buechner and Parker Palmer, respectively: "Listen to your life" and "Let your life speak." I suspect this was Paul's experience in a telescoped way on the Road to Damascus and the following weeks of study and reflection.

We discover our calling through this dynamic interplay of listening and sharing. I believe God speaks to us through every moment of our lives in dramatic and undramatic ways, in casual meetings that hide deeper purposes, off-hand remarks that change the course of our lives, and moments of confession and decision, when we realize that fidelity means transformation, choosing one path rather than other as we walk the talk of the faith we affirm.

In this practice, take time to pause twice each day. In the morning, pause to listen and be still as you open to insight within and beyond yourself, that still small voice spoken in sighs too deep for words. Perhaps, you might ask to experience God's presence in daily activities and to be guided by God's wisdom in your decisions and encounters. A simple prayer, based on the African American spiritual can serve as a touchstone for the day ahead:

> Guide my feet upon the way.
> Open my eyes throughout the day.
> Guide the words I'm about to say.
> Let me walk in Jesus' Way.

Transforming Affirmations

Affirmations redefine our lives and perception of the world. As we move into new and faithful identities, we discover new names to describe ourselves: the weak become strong, the lazy become energetic, the wayward become focused, the anxious find peace, and the fearful discover courage.

God is calling me to transformation in every encounter.
I live out my vocation as God's beloved child.
I let go of the limitations of the past and open to God's vision for
my future.

Manifesting Mission

Light is meant to shine and guide the paths of others. As a child I often sang, "This little light of mine, I'm gonna let it shine" in Sunday School. The song still inspires me. When we experience God's light, our only true choice is to "pass it on!"

Listening to your life, where do you see God calling you to some new act of compassion or care for the world. We each have unique and diverse callings, but all of them are aimed at healing the world and blessing our companions. As you listen to the still, small voice, where is it leading you? Do any of these touch you?

» Toward Earth – care and response to global climate change
» Toward the care of children in person as well as through public policy
» Toward care of single and unmarried mothers
» Toward helping new parents learn parenting skills
» Toward hospitality to immigrants and concern for wise and compassionate public policy
» Toward the unemployed
» Toward the vulnerable and forgotten
» Toward marginalized people through friendship and support of human rights

The list goes on. Every moment can be a call, like Jesus' call to Peter – and later Paul – "follow me on my holy adventure."

NINE

FAITHFUL DISOBEDIENCE

In Caesarea there was a man named Cornelius, a centurion of the Italian Cohort, as it was called. ²He was a devout man who feared God with all his household; he gave alms generously to the people and prayed constantly to God. ³One afternoon at about three o'clock he had a vision in which he clearly saw an angel of God coming in and saying to him, "Cornelius." ⁴He stared at him in terror and said, "What is it, Lord?" He answered, "Your prayers and your alms have ascended as a memorial before God. ⁵Now send men to Joppa for a certain Simon who is called Peter; ⁶he is lodging with Simon, a tanner, whose house is by the seaside." ⁷When the angel who spoke to him had left, he called two of his slaves and a devout soldier from the ranks of those who served him, ⁸and after telling them everything, he sent them to Joppa.

⁹ About noon the next day, as they were on their journey and approaching the city, Peter went up on the roof to pray. ¹⁰He became hungry and wanted something to eat; and while it was being prepared, he fell into a trance. ¹¹He saw the heaven opened and something like a large sheet coming down, being lowered to the ground by its four corners. ¹²In it were all kinds of four-footed creatures and reptiles and birds of the air. ¹³Then he heard a voice saying, "Get up, Peter; kill and eat." ¹⁴But Peter said, "By no means, Lord; for I have never eaten anything that is profane or unclean." ¹⁵The voice said to him again, a second time, "What God has made clean, you must not call profane." ¹⁶This happened three times, and the thing was suddenly taken up to heaven.

¹⁷ Now while Peter was greatly puzzled about what to make of the vision that he had seen, suddenly the men sent by Cornelius appeared. They were asking for Simon's house and were standing by the gate. ¹⁸They called out to ask whether Simon, who was called Peter, was staying there. ¹⁹While Peter was still thinking about the vision, the Spirit said to him, "Look, three men are searching for you. ²⁰Now get up, go down, and go with them without hesitation; for I have sent them." ²¹So Peter went down to the men and said, "I am the one you are looking for; what is the reason for your coming?" ²²They answered, "Cornelius, a centurion, an upright and God-fearing man, who is well spoken of by the whole Jewish nation, was directed by a holy angel to send for you to come to his house and to hear what you have to say." ²³So Peter invited them in and gave them lodging.

[When Peter entered Cornelius' house] *he said to them, "You yourselves know that it is unlawful for a Jew to associate with or to visit a Gentile; but God has shown me that I should not call anyone profane or unclean. So when I was sent for, I came without objection. Now may I ask why you sent for me?"....Gentiles Hear the Good News[After Cornelius shared about his vision] Peter began to speak to them: "I truly understand that God shows no partiality, but in every nation anyone who fears him and does what is right is acceptable to him."....*

While Peter was still speaking, the Holy Spirit fell upon all who heard the word. The circumcised believers who had come with Peter were astounded that the gift of the Holy Spirit had been poured out even on the Gentiles, after they heard them speaking in tongues and extolling God. Then Peter said, "Can anyone withhold the water for baptizing these people who have received the Holy Spirit just as we have?" So he ordered them to be baptized in the name of Jesus Christ. (Acts 10:1-23, 27-28, 34-35, 44-48)

An Unexpected Vision

Have you ever imagined that being hungry would lead to an encounter with God? As the story goes, Peter is waiting for lunch, typically the big meal of the day, and is beginning to drift off to sleep, perhaps, lulled to sleep by the sea air and the sound of waves. To his amazement, he falls into a trance, in which he receives a life-changing vision. Maybe he was just hungry, and he experienced a drop in blood sugar, but God comes to us in our concrete world of possibilities and problems, even temperature and physiology, giving us insights that change our attitudes and enlarge our visions, whether awake or asleep, full or hungry. What God tells him defies everything he believes, but in following God's improbable vision, Peter plays a role in changing the course of Christian history. The circle of grace expands to include Gentiles, and give birth to a global faith.

In Central Pennsylvania, where I lived for several years, people like to eat! There are smorgasbords aplenty in Amish Country – Plain and Fancy, Good and Plenty, and of course the King of Smorgasbords, Shady Maple, boasting over one hundred home-cooked selections.

I imagine that Peter had a vision of a first-century smorgasbord, an all you can eat affair. As he reviewed the feast, I suspect, he was initially delighted to see all kinds of fish and olives, figs and apricots, and good bread and the best wine, but then, he saw something that offended him – shrimp, lobster, and country ham. He is further scandalized when he hears the voice of God inviting him to "kill some of these animals and then come to the table and eat all you want." Peter protests once, twice, and then again, a third time, affirming his orthodoxy and its prohibition of shell fish and pork. He no doubt demands an explanation from the Lawgiver in the Sky, but God challenges him with the admonition "call nothing unclean. Take and eat. Everything's going to be alright!" To Peter's surprise, God is anything but orthodox.

As in the case of Paul's Damascus Road experience, this story describes a "double vision" that surprises both of its recipients. Cornelius, a foreigner, and Roman military leader, impressed by the wisdom of Jewish spirituality, also has a vision, commanding him to send emissaries to Peter's house. He is amazed and grateful that God has heard his prayers, and immediately sends his most trusted employees to Peter's seaside residence.

God, you see, never works solely in solitude. Though God addresses each of us personally, God is the greatest example of the dynamic interdependence of life. Quietly but wisely, God moves through all the intersections of life to provide the wisdom and resources we need to be faithful to our personal and communal vocations. Long before ecology became a household word, the scriptures describe God bringing people together in surprising and synchronous encounters to experience and share God's vision of wholeness and salvation. Although they are strangers, Peter and Cornelius are joined in God's dynamic and interdependent ecology of grace.

Peter awakens from his vision, confused by God's message and, perhaps, feeling a little guilty for partaking in "imaginary" pork and shellfish. But in a few minutes, everything makes sense to the apostle: he hears a knock at the door, welcomes the foreigners, and discovers first-hand that no one is unclean in God's eyes. God shows no partiality but opens the doors of salvation and insight to everyone regardless of ethnicity and social standing.

FAITHFUL DISOBEDIENCE

Peter discovers that he must push his spiritual boundaries and theological dogmas to the limit to be faithful to God. He must disobey the laws of his faith – the theology and ethics he learned as a child and followed as an adult – to follow God's vision for today. He must widen the circle of grace, breaking down boundaries of insider and outsider and clean and unclean, to be faithful to God's grace in a pluralistic and expanding world.

Imagine disobeying God to be faithful to God. But, imagine something even wilder: God changing the rules to fit a new situation. As the United Church of Christ's motto says, "God is still speaking." God never stands still nor does God look backward. Nothing God does is abstract and irrelevant. When times change, God changes, and we trust that God has had a hand in the changes that often disorient us. Leaning forward toward wholeness, God invites us to be forward-looking as well.

PARENTING AND PROVIDENCE

God is a good and faithful parent. God's love for us is unchanging, God is ever-faithful – but, as Lamentations states, God's mercies are new every morning. In fact, God's fidelity is reflected in God's constant innovation and interaction in relationship to the changes in our world. Providence is never timeless but always active in the affairs of persons, nations, and our planet Earth.

Have you noticed that a good parent is always faithful and always changing? Think of the various "rules" parents apply in raising their children. I am relearning this with my toddler grandson, who is always into everything and capable of bolting into the street without warning. His parents and I give him rules and limits for his own – and our own – good: "Don't go in the street"; "Don't touch the computer while grandpa's writing," "Don't push the phone buttons" (he has called 911 twice!), and "Always hold my hand when we walk on the sidewalk." But, what if I gave him this same advice when he's ten years old or on his wedding day? Or, told him "Don't talk to strangers" when he goes away to college? New situations bring new rules and responsibilities for divine and human parents. Or, as our Reformation parents proclaimed, "The reformation is always reforming." Fidelity to God means that we change our strategies and behaviors to share good news in a changing world.

This is not relativism, or an unprincipled faith, but faith that is real as this morning's paper and tomorrow's web technology. The source of order is also the source of novelty. God's creative dislocation, manifested in provocative possibilities and innovative challenges, may initially leave us feeling disoriented – just ask Moses how he felt after hearing the voice of a burning bush, Mary after an angelic visitor, Joseph her fiancé after hearing Mary's news and then encountering an angel in a dream, Paul on the road to Damascus, and Peter on a seaside roof top! Disorientation isn't the end of story. God provides a pathway of possibilities and the energy for new adventures that take us to new landscapes of mission and good news sharing.

Awakening to a Vision

God's disorienting and transforming visions are given to in-dividuals but also communities. In the biblical tradition – and especially in Acts – visions are meant to be shared and embodied in the flesh and blood world of suffering and searching.

If you take the encounter of Peter and Cornelius seriously, it will change your life and change your church. Awakening to a vision often involves a commitment to following spiritual practices within the life of the church and its members. First, awakening to God's vision calls us to prayer, not just when we're hungry, but at all times. Our Native American friends speak of "crying for a vision." The scriptures say that without a vision, the people perish. We need to pray for God's evolving guidance. We need to ask con-stantly: "What new thing does God want us to do to be faithful in our time?" And then we need to listen and ponder what emerges.

Second, seeking a personal and congregational vision means that we should welcome, rather than fear certain changes, even if they unsettle us at first. Peter was unsettled by his vision, until he discovered that God was calling him to a larger faith. What are the changes that your congregation needs to embrace to be faithful to God's call today? Many congregations need to share their good news with the best technology possible and in ways that touch seekers and strangers. Our church websites need to reach out to young adults as well as older seekers and church shoppers. We need to find appropriate ways to share our worship and programs on line, use Facebook, and have regular faith-sharing blogs or online devotions to reach out to new generations.

Third, opening to God's vision means that we should be prayerfully innovative in worship, program, and welcome. What new ways or times of worship do we need to embody? How do we innovatively reach out to people who pass by our churches each week, many from different cultural backgrounds? This may mean change, but remember that once upon a time, "the old time reli-gion" was seen as new-fangled by traditionalists of earlier times.

To many people, Luther's hymn *A Mighty Fortress is Our God* is the quintessential traditional hymn. According to some accounts, when Martin Luther put the words of *A Mighty Fortress* to a popular German song, often sung in bars, he was criticized for being sacrilegious. In response, the Reformer quipped, "Why should the Devil get all the good songs?" This doesn't mean churches should jettison their current worship and music, especially if traditional worship is heart-felt. Still, we can explore other ways of using media and music in worship that embraces all the senses, perhaps even at other times of the week. We can share – and discover – God's good news in hip-hop and rap, heavy metal and grunge music, classical and pop, and poetry and body prayer. Young people and their elders often experience the holy in movies like the *Hunger Games*, *Life is Beautiful*, *The Blind Side*, and other media. Just think of the media that has transformed your way of looking at things and then open to the many pathways of divine revelation across history and across age groups.

Finally, crying for God's vision begs the question: Where do we need to push our theological and hospitality comfort zones? This varies from community to community. But, as the saying goes, "make no small plans" because God has no small plans, and when God gives us a vision, God also provides resources to follow through.

Today, God is still working in our lives and in our world, inviting us personally and as communities toward new visions of faithfulness. These new directions will always challenge us at first. But oh the places we shall go and oh the adventures we will have, when we follow the new pathways God is planning for us.

TRANSFORMING ACTS

Opening to the Spirit

Brother Lawrence speaks of practicing the presence of God. By this he meant a constant intentionality to place each moment in God's care, constantly – and often – unconsciously, asking for God's guidance in every situation. Another spiritual classic, the Russian Orthodox *Way of the Pilgrim*, ponders what it means to pray without ceasing (I Thessalonians 5:17) as he commits himself to saying the Jesus Prayer – "Lord, Jesus Christ, have mercy upon me, a sinner" – with every breath.[1]

While we may not be as disciplined as these two monks, we can commit ourselves throughout the day to asking for God's guidance. We will no doubt find ourselves in disorienting and spiritually spiritually-transforming situations once we set our hearts on God's vision for each moment of our lives. To be specific, we use variations of the following:

> » Guide me to what is best in this situation.
> » Open my eyes to your vision for my life.
> » Awaken me to your wisdom throughout this day.

In this spirit, we might also open to God's many pathways of revelation by asking people of different generations where they are experiencing holiness, inspiration, and ethical guidance, and then take time to listen to, what for you may be novel paths to God.

Transforming Affirmations

Peter discovered two spiritual affirmations after his seaside vision:

> » Everything and everyone God has created is clean and good.
> » God shows no partiality but welcomes everyone to God's realm.

---

1 For more on practicing the presence of God in congregational leadership, see Bruce and Katherine Epperly, *Tending to the Holy: The Practice of the Presence of God in Ministry* (Herndon, VA: Alban, 2009).

God's creative dislocation invites us to ponder our own spiritual affirmations as we confront the holy otherness of God's beloved children. Let me suggest the following affirmations to expand your vision of grace:

God's love embraces all humans, despite their diversity in age, sexuality, ethnicity, and previous behavior.

> *I welcome all of God's children with loving care.*
> *God calls me to service through encounters with strangers.*

Manifesting Mission

Peter's visionary experiences challenges and convicts us. It begs the questions: Who would not be welcome at our church? Who is not worth our time and trouble? What persons or neighborhoods are off-limits for our compassion?

Christian communities often live by pre-set limitations and rules that define insiders and outsiders. Many communities are so sure that they know God's law that they fail to minister to vulnerable and marginalized people. While we need to institute wise and effective immigration policies, many congregants have aligned themselves with alienating and racist public policies rather than welcoming immigrants as God's beloved children. Regardless of the legal issues involved, and our political positions, we must repent of our disregard of the well-being of undocumented immigrants. Regardless of where we've come from, we are welcome at Jesus' table of grace.

After examining our congregation's outreach to strangers, we need to make commitments to inclusion of refugees, homeless persons, and vulnerable elders and children. God speaks through them to awaken us to wider vistas of graceful hospitality. As a congregation's marquee states, we are a church "where all are pilgrims, and none are strangers."

TEN

BELIEVING, BEHAVING, BELONGING

Then certain individuals came down from Judea and were teach-
ing the brothers, "Unless you are circumcised according to the custom
of Moses, you cannot be saved." ²And after Paul and Barnabas had no
small dissension and debate with them, Paul and Barnabas and some of
the others were appointed to go up to Jerusalem to discuss this question
with the apostles and the elders. ³So they were sent on their way by the
church, and as they passed through both Phoenicia and Samaria, they
reported the conversion of the Gentiles, and brought great joy to all the
believers. ⁴When they came to Jerusalem, they were welcomed by the
church and the apostles and the elders, and they reported all that God
had done with them. ⁵But some believers who belonged to the sect of the
Pharisees stood up and said, "It is necessary for them to be circumcised
and ordered to keep the law of Moses."

⁶The apostles and the elders met together to consider this matter.
⁷After there had been much debate, Peter stood up and said to them,
"My brothers, you know that in the early days God made a choice
among you, that I should be the one through whom the Gentiles would
hear the message of the good news and become believers. ⁸And God,
who knows the human heart, testified to them by giving them the Holy
Spirit, just as he did to us; ⁹and in cleansing their hearts by faith he
has made no distinction between them and us. ¹⁰Now therefore why
are you putting God to the test by placing on the neck of the disciples
a yoke that neither our ancestors nor we have been able to bear? ¹¹On
the contrary, we believe that we will be saved through the grace of the
Lord Jesus, just as they will." ¹²The whole assembly kept silence, and
listened to Barnabas and Paul as they told of all the signs and wonders

that God had done through them among the Gentiles. ¹³After they
finished speaking, James replied, "My brothers, listen to me. ¹⁴Simeon
has related how God first looked favorably on the Gentiles, to take from
among them a people for his name…. ¹⁹Therefore I have reached the
decision that we should not trouble those Gentiles who are turning to
God, ²⁰but we should write to them to abstain only from things polluted
by idols and from fornication and from whatever has been strangled
and from blood. ²¹For in every city, for generations past, Moses has had
those who proclaim him." (Acts 15:1-12, 19-21)

HOLISTIC SPIRITUALITY

Although they may differ in describing the temporal sequence
and significance in the lives of individuals and communities, sociol-
ogists and church leaders alike recognize that believing, behaving,
and belonging are at the heart of a person's participation in any
community's life – whether it be a nation, organization, or congregation. While these are dynamically interrelated, fluid, and subject
to evolution and change:

» *Believing* relates to some common understanding or
shared vision of the world, human life, and the purpose
of the organization to which we belong. As Christians,
we may believe various things and even differ on certain
doctrines, but the heart of our faith is our relationship
with and understanding of Jesus Christ and his message
of salvation and wholeness for us today.

» *Behaving* describes a commitment to central practices of
an organization, its mores, and spoken or unspoken codes
of conduct. For example, my wife and mother-in-law are
members of a women's philanthropic organization, PEO.
Although outsiders aren't allowed in group meetings, I have
been told that each meeting has a certain structure and
certain words are said. Christians also have practices that
define who we are. While they differ from place to place

and most of us fall short of the ideal just as we occasionally choose to break traffic laws related to posted speed limits, most Christians pray, serve, welcome strangers, celebrate communion, and worship. While our beliefs may shape our understanding of prayer, commitment to a life of prayer, connecting with the living God, can change our understanding of the world and deepen our beliefs.

» *Belonging* pertains to our commitment to an organization, family, or congregation. When we belong to a community, we make a commitment to its well-being and live by its mission. We go to church, we attend youth group, we stick around for coffee and conversation, and we support the mission with time, talent, and treasure. It matters that we are part of the group: we reach out to others and others support us with kind words, congratulations, casseroles, and companionship in life's struggles. Although some communities depend on coercion and shunning of those who color outside the lines or question the community's values or beliefs, Christian community at its best involves give and take that promotes feelings of safety and support.

TIES THAT BIND

As a child growing up in the Baptist church, we always sang *Blest Be the Ties that Bind* as the closing hymn on Communion Sundays.

Blest be the tie that binds
    Our hearts in Christian love;
    The fellowship of kindred minds
    Is like to that above.
Before our Father's throne
    We pour our ardent prayers;
    Our fears, our hopes, our aims are one
    Our comforts and our cares.
We share each other's woes,
    Our mutual burdens bear;

And often for each other flows
The sympathizing tear.

These words, along with Sunday School, church picnics, worship, friendships, and common prayer defined the contours of faith to me as a child. They still shape my understanding of church and its mission. But, such fellowship is a matter of daily practice and can be easily lost when we place our personal beliefs and values along with unbending adherence of our traditions ahead of God's call to beloved communities of Shalom.

The relationship of believing, behaving, and belonging became paramount in the early church. The first followers of Jesus wrestled as the church expanded with the questions: What happens to our beliefs and community when we open the borders to everyone? What happens when you leave the doors of tradition unlocked and let new ideas and ways of doing things come in? What happens when everyone is welcome just as they are – diverse in ethnicity, ethics, diet, lifestyle, and language? These are serious questions because personal and communal identity require a healthy blend of order and novelty, tradition and change, and uniformity and diversity.

Certain Christians found the rapidly growing and quickly evolving faith of the Jesus movement threatening to their understanding of the interplay of belief, behavior, and belonging. "Everybody's welcome regardless of ethnicity and lifestyle," they complained. "But, remember we are the followers of a Jewish teacher, and that means we must follow the Jewish laws: males must be circumcised and everyone must eat, behave, and work in accordance with a strict understanding of the laws of Moses." Some were so ardent about teaching a Jewish form of Christianity to the Gentile believers that they monitored Paul's and perhaps Peter's visits to new Gentile churches and as soon as the apostles left, they showed up with the intention of setting the new Christians straight, and repudiating the Christian freedom that was at the heart of Paul's message and evidently affirmed by Peter's new found hospitality to Gentiles.

The Christian movement might have been on the verge of splitting into two clear factions – a Gentile church and a Jewish church. Do you remember the sad days of American Christianity in which African Americans were required to sit in balconies while their white brothers and sisters sat in the main sanctuary? Despite all the talk of Christian love by their white masters and employers, persons of African descent were considered second-class Christians, unworthy of direct contact with their white brothers and sisters.

The same dynamic was at work in the relationship of Jewish and Gentile Christians. Following Jesus meant living as you always did for Jewish Christians. Jewish Christians didn't have to alter their behavior and life-style to belong to the new community of faith. But, according to the traditionalists, admission of Gentiles as full members of the community required changes in behavior, lifestyle, and I suspect a good deal of inconvenience and pain for adult males. Gentiles would have to renounce their customs and ethnicity to become full-fledged Christians. Sadly, this same phenomenon reappeared in the nineteenth and twentieth century global mission movements. Many indigenous Christians were virtually compelled to adopt Western practices in worship, dress, and language to be recognized as practitioners of the one, true faith. Their cultures were considered impediments, rather than resources, for following Jesus. Their language and way of life were scorned as "primitive" and "godless" by many European and North American missionaries and the business people and political leaders who came with them. Only recently has this cultural imperialism been abandoned, enabling world Christianity to become a creative and lively synthesis of unity of allegiance to Christ and diversity of culture, practice, sacrament, and understanding of God's work in the world. After all, if God is omnipresent, then God's wisdom shaped indigenous cultures long before Europeans brought the message of Jesus Christ to them.

At the Jerusalem Council, Peter and Paul challenge these requirements: they believe that placing requirements on the Gentile Christians make grace something Gentiles have to earn and not a free gift of God. They place a burden on Gentile Christians that is not asked of Jewish Christians.

While I suspect the Jerusalem Council didn't solve all the problems of insider and outsider status, it built the foundation for the spread of Christianity across the globe by it making it possible for non-ethnic Jews to become first class Christians.

Paul and Peter were motivated by a dynamic understanding of believing, belonging, and behaving. They believed that God's grace and the coming of the Spirit were at the heart of the Jesus movement. Persons don't have to earn God's love: it comes to us at our best and at our worst. We simply need to reach out and say "yes" to the love that's given us.

For the Jerusalem Council, behaving involved most of all love and generosity, and giving the grace that they received. Faith involves a changed lifestyle: in a society in which promiscuity was accepted. The first Gentile Christians were challenged to stand apart by faithful sexuality, generosity to one another beyond their families, and abstention from food that had been polluted in the pagan temples. Frankly, these requirements were essential for preserving community identity and healthy relationships.

Now, there is no royal road to living out this holy trinity of believing, behaving, and belonging. Some people belong before they believe – they hang around a church or Christians and find themselves feeling at home spiritually. They find a community where they matter and where they can make a difference. Others learn a prayer practice or reach out to the vulnerable and discover God in the process. Still others find a God they can believe in – not like the God preached in their childhood congregation or on television – and then a congregation that reflects their faith journey and nurtures them theologically and spiritually.

Inclusion, Ethics, and Transformation

Our pluralistic postmodern age challenges the church to take this holy trinity of believing, behaving, and belonging seriously. Openness to religious diversity, ironically, demands thorough, but fluid, understanding of our own tradition. Many congregations see theological reflection as optional. Community and social action are sufficient for Christian life, they assert. In contrast, I believe that in a world of seekers and other religious traditions, we need to be able to share what we believe and how our beliefs have made a difference in our lives. Cultivating a sound theology, or putting together a flexible theological vision, enables us to enter into dialogue with others and face the challenges of failure, disease, aging, and death with a sense of meaning and trust in God's care for us and those we love. Our faith matures when we read scripture, devotional books, and accessible theological texts.

Jesus' first followers were often described as People of the Way. Following their pattern will discover that faithfulness to Jesus involves a way of life, characterized by prayer, generosity, hospitality, forgiveness, and service to the broader community and the planet.

Radical hospitality requires both intimacy and intentionality. Having an open door doesn't mean anything goes. In fact, the more open you are to diversity of belief and lifestyle, the more intentional your structures of community need to be: we need to have covenants that help us behave as Christians as well as create a safe place for diversity, disagreement, and doubt, not to mention the well-being of everyone in this church, including the children. Christian love is sacrificial and generous but generosity requires flexible structures of grace: my generation remembers that line from the film "Love Story" – "love is never having to say you're sorry." Well, that isn't the love of the gospels: love is looking out for each other, going the second mile to insure someone gets to church or finds help in a job search or comfort in the hospital, or keeping our eyes open to unhealthy behaviors and working compassionately to challenge each other to be our most Christ-like self. Love may on occasion mean heart-felt apology and confession, but it always means forgiveness and willingness to give others a second chance.

Sojourners has recently released a film on poverty called *The Line*. In the context of the 2012 US Presidential Election, one advertisement states "Matthew 25 doesn't say as you have done unto the middle class you have done unto me!"[1] Acts of the Apostles portrays the early Christians' struggle to be faithful to the teachings of Jesus, the Pentecost experience, and the gift of the Spirit to Gentiles. If we claim that the Spirit of God is available to everyone, then everyone is welcome at God's banquet table. Paul captured the universality of welcome in his words to the Christians in Galatia, some of whom were treated as second class citizens because of their ethnicity:

> *As many of you as were baptized into Christ have clothed your-selves with Christ.*
> [28] *There is no longer Jew or Greek, there is no longer slave or free, there is no longer male and female; for all of you are one in Christ Jesus.* [29] *And if you belong to Christ, then you are Abraham's offspring, heirs according to the promise.* (Galatians 3:27-29)

Every division and temptation to polarize is challenged as irrelevant to God's good news of salvation in Jesus Christ. Christ moves through all the diversities of our world. "For neither circumcision or uncircumcision means anything; but a new creation is everything" (Galatians 6:15)!

Many of us remember the television comedy *Cheers*. In contrast to the anonymity of many churches, for whom strangers are as much an inconvenience as an opportunity, this Boston bar was one place in a world of isolation "where everybody knows your name." Belonging means finding a home where people welcome you, respect you, hear your voice, and know your name. The ministries of Peter and Paul achieved more than the apostles could imagine

---

1 http://sojo.net/blogs/2012/09/06/watch-line-most-important-film-youll-see-year

theologically and behaviorally. If the church truly welcomes persons of other races, economic situations, and lifestyles, then the church must listen to its members in the same way a healthy body is shaped by all its cells. Opening to diversity means willingness to change and hospitality leads to the transformation of worship services, mission statements, and leadership. To be faithful to God, we – like the first Christians – must intentionally choose a dynamic and careful balance of tradition and innovation and unity and diversity. That's what new creation is all about!

TRANSFORMING ACTS

Opening to the Spirit

In this spiritual exercise, you are invited to look for the light of God in everyone you see. Begin with a time of quiet, breathing gently and slowly. After a few minutes, visualize a healing light flowing in you with every breath, let it radiate through you from the top of your head to the soles of your feet and then surround you in a protective armor of light. Permeated and protected by God's presence, take some time to visualize your "outsiders" – whether personal, social, or political. Begin to see them as surrounded by God's light and as God's beloved children. Experience God's light shining in and through them. Conclude by asking God to enable you to see the light in everyone you meet.

Throughout the day, look for the light in people you meet, especially those who you perceive as disagreeable or alien as a result of behavior, political views, or physical and mental health condition.

Seeing the light in another does not mean accepting unacceptable behavior or supporting their political policies; it simply means a willingness to withhold prejudices, projections, and polarizing. It means looking for the light rather than darkness in them. Even when we challenge others' behaviors, our responses to them are grounded in our awareness of God's grace, which joins all of us, imperfect yet loved.

Transforming Affirmations

Every one of us needs a transformed vision. Jesus said, "You are the light of the world," and challenged us to let our light shine. Jesus' words challenge us also to see God's light shining through the prisms of diversity, honoring differences and recognizing the holiness of "otherness."

I am the light of the world. God's light shines through me to others.
In God's light, I see light in the darkest place.
I welcome diversity and learn from many voices and cultures.

Manifesting Mission

The Jerusalem Council is a timeless event and a contextual reality. We are always navigating diverse theological and ethical positions, cultural viewpoints, and lifestyle and ethnic differences. There is always a temptation to see others as second-class and beyond the circle of grace. We easily look down on those who hold different political, ethical, and lifestyle positions and assume a privileged position. They must become like us, believe like us, and behave like us to be accepted into our circle. The recent USA political crises and governmental gridlock and polarization reflect an inability on the part of certain political leaders to see truth in contrasting persons or value in leaders from ethnic groups. Caught up in their own "principles," they cannot imagine that others are motivated by good will and the best interest of our country. We need to ask forgiveness for our implicit racism, sexism, and fear of otherness along with our unwillingness to change for the good of the community.

We need to put this healing vision into practice by reaching out to persons with whom we disagree in quest of common ground. We must see God in the least of these, especially the "least" who oppose us theologically, politically, or socially. Even if we don't come to an agreement, reaching out is an antidote to the life-destroying alienation and polarization characteristic of our times.

ELEVEN

How Can We Keep from Singing!

One day, as we were going to the place of prayer, we met a slave-girl who had a spirit of divination and brought her owners a great deal of money by fortune-telling. [17]*While she followed Paul and us, she would cry out, "These men are slaves of the Most High God, who proclaim to you* a way of salvation."* [18]*She kept doing this for many days. But Paul, very much annoyed, turned and said to the spirit, "I order you in the name of Jesus Christ to come out of her." And it came out that very hour.*

[19]*But when her owners saw that their hope of making money was gone, they seized Paul and Silas and dragged them into the market-place before the authorities.* [20]*When they had brought them before the magistrates, they said, "These men are disturbing our city; they are Jews* [21]*and are advocating customs that are not lawful for us as Romans to adopt or observe."* [22]*The crowd joined in attacking them, and the magistrates had them stripped of their clothing and ordered them to be beaten with rods.* [23]*After they had given them a severe flogging, they threw them into prison and ordered the jailer to keep them securely.* [24]*Following these instructions, he put them in the innermost cell and fastened their feet in the stocks.* [25]*About midnight Paul and Silas were praying and singing hymns to God, and the prisoners were listening to them.* (Acts 16:16-25)

THE POWER OF AFFIRMATIVE FAITH

Throughout our adventures through Acts of the Apostles, I have asserted that what we believe shapes our actions and how we respond to the events of our lives. Our deepest convictions about the nature of things and about God enable us to face crises with calm and reach outsiders, claiming them as brothers and sisters in Christ. How we understand the world and our relationship to God not only shapes our character and the way we behave when no one's looking and guides our aspirations, it also enables us to respond to what we cannot change, including the challenges and tragedies that are part of even a good life. Our character is formed day by day by our affirmations of faith and actions.[1]

Scott Peck begins his best-selling book *The Road Less Traveled* with the words, "Life is Difficult." Amid the beauty of life, every one of us must eventually walk through the valley of the shadow. C. S. Lewis notes that just as falling in love is part of every relationship, bereavement or grief is a season of every marriage that no couple can avoid. In a course of a lifetime, we face events we never would have chosen – even for our enemies – a child with cancer, job loss and economic reversal, betrayal, and the inevitable aging process and the reality of death. Further, the mortality rate remains and will remain at 100% despite medical advances in promoting longevity and curing once fatal diseases. How we respond to these events can deepen our faith or destroy us; it can enhance our appreciation of the beauty of life or embitter us.

WHEN TROUBLE COMES OUR WAY

Paul is once again in trouble. He is reaching out to the new church in Philippi (in today's Macedonia, north of Greece), gathering a truly inclusive community of faithful believers meeting at the home of Lydia, a prosperous merchant. He is hounded daily by a slave girl, a psychic, who accurately identifies him as a servant of Jesus. Finally – and this is strange motivation for performing a healing – Paul gets so annoyed by her that he heals her of the spirit possession from which her psychic powers emerge. Her owners are

1 For more on the relationship of spiritual affirmations to personal growth and conduct, see Bruce Epperly, *Holy Adventure: 41 Days of Audacious Living* (Nashville: Upper Room, 2008).

rightfully angry, according to their materialistic value system. After all, he's interfering with commerce and capitalism. They have Paul arrested, beaten, and tossed in jail. But in jail, Paul and his fellow missionary Silas do something unexpected, they pray and sing. "At midnight they were praying and singing songs to God and the other prisoners were listening."

Singing songs in prison? Rejoicing in the hospital? Giving thanks at the graveside? Looking for possibilities amid failure? Or new routes when the old ways no longer work? Opening to love despite heartbreak? That is what it means to sing and pray in prison and to recognize that whether we find ourselves in the heights or depths, God is with us!

In psychiatrist Victor Frankl's account of imprisonment in the Nazi concentration camps. *Man's Search for Meaning*, he notes that everything can be taken away from a person except her or his ability to shape their response to the events of her or his life. Despite the circumstances of life, we still have the freedom to choose our attitude. That is what Paul and Silas did as they raised their voices behind prison bars!

Singing in prison sounds a little Pollyanna-ish, doesn't it? Sort of a "look on the sunny side, praise the Lord anyway" approach to life, that denies the real pain we feel and the realities of suffering in our world. But, the fictional character Pollyanna gets a bad rap. Throughout her difficult life, she was optimistic and hopeful, not unrealistic. She saw a deeper realism, beneath the limitations and pain of life that placed life's problems in a larger, more creative and hopeful perspective.

Perhaps you've read the story or seen the movie, *Pollyanna*. After losing both her parents, Pollyanna Whittier comes to live in Beldingsville, Vermont, with her wealthy but stern Aunt Polly. This young girl lives by the principles of the "The Glad Game," a hopeful approach toward life she learned from her father. The game is played by finding something to be glad about in every situation, even personal disappointments and reversals. Pollyanna learned it one Christmas when she was hoping for a doll in the missionary barrel of gifts for needy families, but found only a pair of crutches inside. Despite their poverty, her father invited her to look on the bright side of life, reminding her to be glad about the crutches because "we didn't need to use them!"

Years later, Pollyanna had to draw on this same faith when she was paralyzed after being hit by a car: the witnesses of people who had been transformed by her attitude restored her spirit and enabled her to walk again.

FAITH THAT SINGS

It has been said that when you sing, you pray twice! What inspired Paul, Silas, and Pollyanna was an imaginative vision of life, based on their experience and trust in God's providential care. You could call it a practical theology, experiences and beliefs made flesh in responding to life's challenges. Beaten and in pain, Paul and Silas could still sing because their lives were guided by a handful of life-changing affirmations that show up throughout Paul's writings:

- » The good work God has begun in my life, He will bring to fullness and it will be a harvest of righteousness (Philippians 1:3-11).
- » If God be for us, who can be against us (Romans 8:36).
- » Nothing can separate us [me] from the love of God in Christ Jesus our savior (Romans 8:38-39).
- » I can do all things through Christ who strengthens me.
- » God is near (Philippians 4:13).
- » My God will supply all my needs through His riches and glory (Philippians 4:18).
- » God's grace is sufficient for me, His power is revealed in our weakness (2 Corinthians 12:9).

I suspect that Paul's and Silas' spirits were also buoyed by the experience that brought them to Philippi in the first place. God had given them a vision and they trusted that if they followed God's pathway, He would give them the resources and energy to respond to anything that stood in their way. Time after time, God had made a way for Paul, where realistically there had been no way forward, beginning with his Damascus Road experience. Paul knew first-hand that God's providence was at work even in prison. While God did not unilaterally put Paul in prison, Paul knew that even in prison, God as at work. Later, he was to write, "In all things God works for good." With Paul, we can assert that while God does not choose cancer, joblessness, bereavement, or physical diminishment for ourselves or those we love, God is there where the pain – and joy – is, giving us energy, strength, courage, and inspiration to make it to the other side.

Cling to Paul's affirmations and your life will be transformed. Remember your personal God-moments and you will find strength. You will face serious challenges and know that you are not alone. You will be guided by love not fear and face what can't be changed when there is hope, knowing that in all things, God is with us. Whether we live or die, we belong to God and God hasn't lost anyone yet!

Let me conclude with a song that has gotten me through some tough times – a child's cancer, the death of my brother and my parents, and the loss of a job when I was at the top of my professional career.

> My life flows on in endless song;
> Above earth's lamentation,
> I hear the sweet, tho' far-off hymn
> That hails a new creation;
> Thro' all the tumult and the strife
> I hear the music ringing;
> It finds an echo in my soul—
> How can I keep from singing?..[1]

There is great meaning in a verse that was added during the persecution of social reformers during the McCarthy era. It reminds

1 Rev. Robert Wadsworth Lowry. *How Can I Keep from Singing?*

me that despite my own temptations and weakness, I aspire to be a person of Christian character and with God's help I will run the race that lies ahead of me:

> When tyrants tremble, sick with fear,
> And hear their death-knell ringing,
> When friends rejoice both far and near,
> How can I keep from singing?
> In prison cell and dungeon vile,
> Our thoughts to them go winging;
> When friends by shame are undefiled,
> How can I keep from singing?[1]

Yes, with God as our companion and source of energy, insight, and freedom, how can we keep from singing?

TRANSFORMING ACTS

Opening to the Spirit

Many of us have found spiritual comfort through song during times of duress. The hymns we sing, whether traditional or contemporary, reflect every season of life from joy to desolation. Some of the great hymns such as *Precious Lord, Take My Hand, It is Well With My Soul,* and *Now Thank We All Our God* were written in times of bereavement. *Amazing Grace* reflects gratitude for God's saving work that embraces moral wretches, lost souls, and spiritually insensitive persons.

What songs have changed your life? What hymns do you return to in times of challenge? What hymns reflect your joy at God's wondrous love and the beauty of life? Take time to pray twice by singing some of these hymns. In addition, you may decide to listen to them on the internet or purchase CDs or downloads.

---

1 Additional words by Doris Plenn.

My Life Goes On (*How Can I Keep From Singing*) has been my spiritual companion during two times of professional crisis. *Great is Thy Faithfulness* filled my heart when my only child was being treated for cancer. *God of Change and Glory* reminds me that life is about praise and gratitude: "For the giver and the gift. Praise! Praise! Praise!" I arise every morning, singing (not so loud as to wake my wife and neighbors), "This is the Day! This is the Day that Our God has Made!"

Throughout the day let you soul sing out its praise and gratitude and trust that through every season of life, God will give us the imagination, energy, and courage to confront injustice, welcome the outsider, and bring joy to our friends and families.

Transforming Affirmations

Sung and spoken affirmations transform our perceptions, self-image, behavior, and even our life situation. As I was typing, my mind went back to my small town Baptist childhood and two hymns that made a difference to a young boy. Do you remember them?

> I sing because I'm happy.
> I sing because I'm free.
> His eye is on the sparrow
> And I know he's watching me.[1]

And

> This is light of mine,
> I'm gonna let it shine.
> This little light of mine,
> I'm gonna let it shine.
> This little light of mine,
> I'm gonna let it shine,
> Let it shine, Let it shine, Let it shine.[2]

---

1 Civilla D. Martin. *His Eye is on the Sparrow.*
2 Henry Dixon Loes. *This Little Light of Mine.*

Now those songs can give a child confidence and worth – just like another childhood hymn – *Jesus Loves Me, This I know.*

What hymn affirmations can *will* change your life? Here are few affirmations for the journey. Feel free to create affirmations based on your own favorite hymns.

I thank God in every situation. (*Now Thank We All Our God*)

I praise God for diversity and adventure. (*God of Change and Glory*)

God is always faithful to me. God's mercies are new every morning.(*Great is Thy Faithfulness*)

Manifesting Mission

Mission joins head, heart, and hands, as well as thought, emotion, and service. Paul and Silas found hope in God's faithful companionship. They knew that God's providence was seeking good even behind prison bars. In response to the grace you have received, your missional calling is to share God's grace with others, most especially persons who appear be trapped by life's circumstances: aging, caring for loved ones, financial distress, illness, incarceration, addiction, violence, or faith crises. At times, people are so overwhelmed that they don't have the energy or insight for the next step. Your challenge is to find creative ways to support them while preserving their integrity and sense of self. This might mean actions such as: home or hospital visitation, help with house cleaning or shopping, listening, encouragement, referral to professional help, and always and everywhere prayer. It might also mean advocacy for fair treatment of prisoners, undocumented immigrants, families on welfare, and the victims of war. As Christians, our service is not accidental but rises from our gratitude for God's abundant love and our calling to share God's love with others, bringing beauty to God and the world.

CHAPTER TWELVE

A GENTLE, PERSISTANT PROVIDENCE

Three months later we set sail on a ship that had wintered at the island, an Alexandrian ship with the Twin Brothers as its figurehead. [12]We put in at Syracuse and stayed there for three days; [13]then we weighed anchor and came to Rhegium. After one day there a south wind sprang up, and on the second day we came to Puteoli. [14]There we found believers and were invited to stay with them for seven days. And so we came to Rome. [15]The believers from there, when they heard of us, came as far as the Forum of Appius and Three Taverns to meet us. On seeing them, Paul thanked God and took courage.

[16] When we came into Rome, Paul was allowed to live by himself, with the soldier who was guarding him.... He lived there for two whole years at his own expense and welcomed all who came to him, proclaiming the kingdom of God and teaching about the Lord Jesus Christ with all boldness and without hindrance. (Acts 28:11-16, 30-31)

A NEVER-ENDING STORY

Acts of the Apostles is, as the title of a children's fantasy film goes, a "Never-ending Story." Though it ends with Paul in prison, its last words – words repeated throughout the text – speak of good news that bursts forth in every challenging situation, good news that pushes us outside of our comfort zones, and invites us to imagine new possibilities and discover the energy to embody them. Paul spent two years, absolutely free despite incarceration, "proclaiming the kingdom of God and teaching about the Lord Jesus Christ with all boldness and without hindrance." Paul's "life flows on in endless song" and the author of Acts of the Apostle, as he records his narrative of the early church, anticipates the message of Jesus Christ and God's realm of Shalom will spread across the globe, throughout the ages, and beyond anything he – or we, twenty-one centuries later – can imagine. Luke didn't know about us, but he did know that his words had the power to transform lives in every generation till the end of history. He isn't concerned with a "second coming" because in the journey from Ascension to Rome, he has discovered that Christ comes to us every moment of the day.

That's the story of Acts of the Apostles – the unhindered gospel, the good news that transformed the first century church and good news that can transform your church, your life, and the world. Like the first followers of Jesus, many of us have experienced this good news. We have survived and thrived eventually after the death of a spouse. We have triumphed after adversity; we have persisted despite pain. We have overcome addictions day by day; and we have learned to love again. We want to tell the world about good news that embraces all creation, healing the sick, restoring spirits, welcoming the lost, embracing outcasts, and promising everlasting life, beginning right now!

PERSISTENT, LOVING PROVIDENCE

Providence can mean a number of different things. To some people, it means that God decides everything and we are simply instruments of God's will, thinking we have freedom, but really puppets of predestination. Whatever happens is God's will and we must submit to it. To other believers, it means that God sends us disease, trauma, and even abuse to strengthen our character and test our resolve. But I suggest another meaning: providence is the movement of God, mostly unnoticed and imperceptible, that guides our days, influences our growth, and works within the events of our lives to support our well-being and the well-being of the world. Providence is not all-determining or punitive, it doesn't test us, but it refines and challenges us in the moment by moment events of our lives. Providence is good news for everyone. God guides our steps even when we are wayward and God will welcome every child home, regardless of far they have strayed.

Providence is at work in a baby's latching on to her mother's breast, in the urge to crawl, in the slow healing of wounds of the body, mind, and spirit, in insights, hunches, and illuminations, in synchronous encounters and dramatic life changes. Providence is equally found in the soft sighs too deep for words in times of grief and questioning as well as the bright light and booming voice on the road to Damascus. As one translation of Romans 8:28 proclaims, "In all things God works for good." The winds of a graceful, guiding Spirit move through our daily struggles, in our job situations and school experiences, in our health conditions and personality types, in the growth toward adulthood and the movement toward aging. God breathes in us, giving us spiritual CPR and a second wind for the adventures ahead.

God doesn't compel or determine our every action or the events of our lives, but works like an artist seeking to bring about the best in every situation and inspire us to become greater, stronger, and more creative than we imagined possible.

We have all experienced the second wind of providence. It might have been in looking across the table and, despite our failures at previous relationships, truly seeing the person you were to spend your life with for the first time and then taking the risk to get to know him or her. It might have been in the urge to see a physician, because you just didn't feel right, and got a diagnosis just in time to avoid a life-threatening incident. It might have been accidentally meeting the person who was to become your spiritual or professional mentor. Providence might have come to you in a touch that healed a broken heart or an anointing that restored your health. Providence comes in mystical experiences and gentle nudges.

Divine providence is gently at work in all things: as Paul was to say in Philippians 1:3-11, "the good work God has begun in your lives God will bring to fullness…. and it will be a harvest of righteousness."[1]

Acts of the Apostles is a testimony to what happens when you open to God's providence: mighty winds blow, inspiration comes, healing energy emerges, Philip meets an Ethiopian, Paul sees a vision, Peter is invited to see the unclean as loved by God, and Paul sings in prison.

I believe there is a gentle providence in life. It doesn't insulate us from job loss, aging, conflict, and death, but it inspires us to be active, hopeful, and creative in response to the events of life. It gives us insight and courage to respond to social justice and claim our role as God's partners in healing the earth.

I suspect that these providential moments abound, often hidden in everyday life and in difficult challenges, but their existence reminds us that there is always a deeper realism, a reality that reveals more than meets the eye – born of a wisdom and power not our own, providing possibilities, insights, and energy; making a way where there was no way.

"Yes" to Adventure

So, I conclude today with one practical piece of advice: keep your eyes open for providential opportunities. Live prayerfully, and when – to quote Yogi Berra – you come to a fork in the road, take it! – that is, claim your power act when decisions need to be made. Don't let failure or disappointment stall you; and be open to something new every day for your church and in your life. The story of Acts is your story. God is still speaking, healing, guiding, transforming, and welcoming. God's providence is an unhindered and never-ending story!

Let me close with the words of Dag Hammarskjold that speak to my feelings for you and trust in the providence that guides us

---

1 For more on the relationship of theology, spirituality, and community in Philippians, see Bruce Epperly, *Philippians: A Participatory Study Guide* (Gonzales, FL: Energion Publications, 2011).

all. Although I mentioned them as part of an exercise in gratitude, highlighted in Chapter Four, they are appropriate as we continue our journey as God's companions in healing the Earth.

> For all that has been – thanks!
> For all that shall be – yes!
> In that "yes" to the Spirit, the future of the world depends!

TRANSFORMING ACTS

Opening to the Spirit

In this final exercise, contemplate once again the words of Dag Hammarskjold, who served as General Secretary of the United Nations. They are at the heart of a living theology and spirituality.

> For all that has been – thanks!
> For all that shall be – yes!

Though we reflected on gratitude earlier in this book, the importance of gratitude as a foundation for ethics and mission needs to be affirmed as we set forth on our spiritual pilgrimages for our time. For what are you most thankful these days? What blessings can you count as an antidote to fear, frustration, and hopelessness? Where have you experienced God's providential love bringing you from darkness to light, and death to life?

Providence is at work in every moment of life – past, present, and future. What great "yes" do you imagine awaiting you? What new possibilities are being born in your life and congregation? Pray for insight to recognize providence and then venture forth on a holy adventure with God's wind at your back!

Transforming Affirmations

God's omnipresent and omni-active love is the source of blessings and insights throughout our lives. Most of the time we don't notice these gentle nudges toward wholeness and mission. Affirmations open our senses and intuition to the graces spread across our pathway.

> *God's providence guides my every step.*
> *In all things God is working for good.*
> *God is giving me the insight and energy to follow my [God's]* dreams.

Manifesting Mission

You could be the answer to someone's prayer. Acts of the Apostles is all about synchronous encounters in which persons showed up at just the right time: Philip and the Ethiopian eunuch, Ananias and Paul, Peter and Cornelius, Lydia and Paul, Paul and the Philippian jailer. Earlier in this quest, I quoted Leslie Weatherhead who asserted that "when I pray coincidences happen, when I don't, they don't." There is a providential synchronicity at work in our lives that regularly places us at the right place at the right time. Only occasionally do we notice these life-shaping moments.

Make a commitment to pray regularly to be open to God's leading in relationship with others. The tapestry of God's providence is multi-faceted, interdependent, and intimately connected. God may be nudging you right now to take a certain way home or stop on the way, or linger after a meeting. God also may be quietly luring someone in your direction. In the web of life, God may intend for you to be a messenger of grace to another person. After all, God's providence is unhindered as it invites us to be companions on a never-ending story.

ALSO FROM ENERGION PUBLICATIONS
and Bruce Epperly

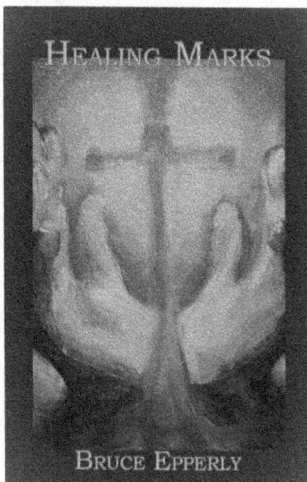

... inspirational, timely, insightful, and wise.

Edwin David Aponte
Vice President for Academic Affairs
Dean of the Faculty and Professor,
Christianity and Culture
Christian Theological Seminary

... a solid presentation of the historical, sociological, and ideological issues that arise from reading Philippians.

Lisa Davison
Professor of Hebrew Bible
Phillips Theological Seminary

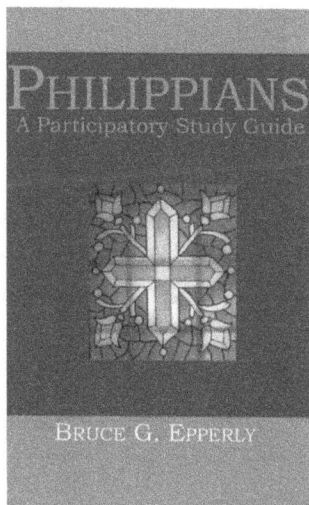

Watch for
Letters to My Grandson
(Coming this fall)

MORE FROM ENERGION PUBLICATIONS

Personal Study

Finding My Way in Christianity	Herold Weiss	$16.99
Holy Smoke! Unholy Fire	Bob McKibben	$14.99
The Jesus Paradigm	David Alan Black	$17.99
When People Speak for God	Henry Neufeld	$17.99
The Sacred Journey	Chris Surber	$11.99

Christian Living

Faith in the Public Square	Robert D. Cornwall	$16.99
Grief: Finding the Candle of Light	Jody Neufeld	$8.99
Crossing the Street	Robert LaRochelle	$16.99

Bible Study

Learning and Living Scripture	Lentz/Neufeld	$12.99
From Inspiration to Understanding	Edward W. H. Vick	$24.99
Luke: A Participatory Study Guide	Geoffrey Lentz	$8.99
Philippians: A Participatory Study Guide	Bruce Epperly	$9.99
Ephesians: A Participatory Study Guide	Robert D. Cornwall	$9.99

Theology

Creation in Scripture	Herold Weiss	$12.99
Creation: the Christian Doctrine	Edward W. H. Vick	$12.99
The Politics of Witness	Allan R. Bevere	$9.99
Ultimate Allegiance	Robert D. Cornwall	$9.99
The Church Under the Cross	William Powell Tuck	$11.99
The Journey to the Undiscovered Country	William Powell Tuck	$9.99
Eschatology: A Participatory Study Guide	Edward W. H. Vick	$9.99

Ministry

Clergy Table Talk	Kent Ira Groff	$9.99
Out of This World	Darren McClellan	$24.99
Healing Marks	Bruce Epperly	$14.99

Generous Quantity Discounts Available
Dealer Inquiries Welcome
Energion Publications — P.O. Box 841
Gonzalez, FL_ 32560
Website: http://energionpubs.com
Phone: (850) 525-3916

www.ingramcontent.com/pod-product-compliance
Lightning Source LLC
LaVergne TN
LVHW041322080426
835513LV00008B/555